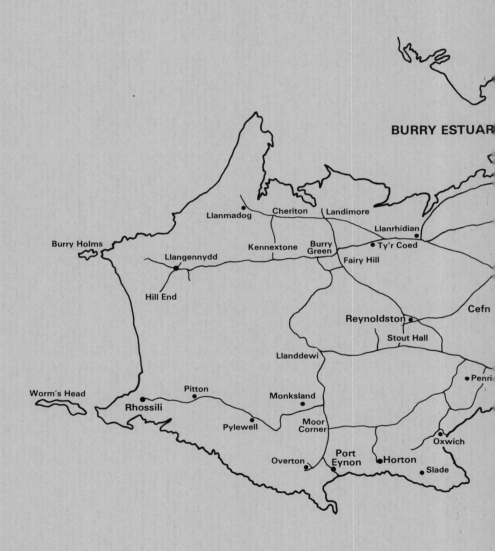

BURRY ESTUAR

Burry Holms

Llanmadog
Cheriton
Landimore
Llanrhidian
Kennextone
Burry
Green
Ty'r Coed
Llangennydd
Fairy Hill
Hill End
Reynoldston
Cefn
Stout Hall
Llanddewi
Penri
Worm's Head
Pitton
Monksland
Rhossili
Pylewell
Moor
Corner
Oxwich
Overton
Port
Eynon
Horton
Slade

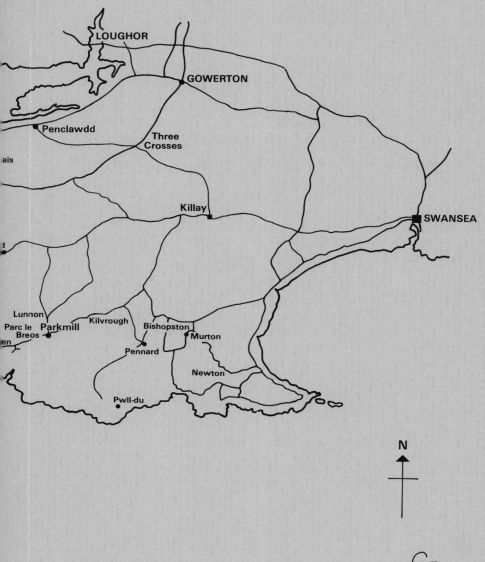

LOUGHOR

GOWERTON

Penclawdd

Three
Crosses

ais

Killay

SWANSEA

Lunnon
Parc le   Parkmill   Kilvrough   Bishopston
Breos   Murton
en
Pennard

Newton

Pwll-du

N

G 81

YESTERDAY'S GOWER

Frontispiece: Bishopston Valley, 1917: author's wife (centre) with mother and twin brother and sister.

Yesterday's Gower

J. Mansel Thomas

GOMER PRESS
1982

First Impression—August 1982

ISBN 0 85088 747 X

©Gwendolen Thomas

Printed by J. D. Lewis & Sons Ltd.,
Gomer Press, Llandysul, Dyfed

FOR HILDEGARDE AND GARETH
AND FOR THEIR FAMILIES

Acknowledgements

I am glad to have this opportunity of thanking all those people who have given me encouragement and practical help during the three years it has taken me to see my husband's book published.

I should particularly mention my brother-in-law, Mr. Glyn Davies, for his advice on matters connected with printing and for the time he has spent on proof-reading. Also I must thank Professor Glanmor Williams for contributing such a perceptive Foreword and for reading the original and the amended manuscripts.

For the illustrations used in this book I am grateful to the people who made available for my use their treasured family photographs and to Valerie Ganz for making the delightful line drawings. I am indebted to the Gower Society for permission to reprint photographs previously published by them, and to the Archives Department of Swansea City Council for their courteous assistance.

Lastly, on Mansel's behalf, my gratitude goes to the Gower people themselves who co-operated so wholeheartedly with him, and welcomed him into their homes. For him each visit deepened his respect and affection for them.

Gwendolen Thomas

Rhossili, July 1982

Contents

Foreword

Mansel Thomas was one of those men endowed with such warm, rich and sympathetic humanity that he made a host of friends. So it is a particular honour and pleasure for me, as one who counted himself among those friends for thirty years, to have been asked to contribute a foreword to this last of his books, which stands as a posthumous memorial to him. Mansel had given much of his life to Gower and its people, and had devoted his unusually sensitive and receptive personality to observing, understanding and loving them. His gentle, discerning, and compassionate temperament made him a superb listener, with a singularly rare gift for encouraging others to converse with him and confide in him. An exceptionally talented author, he wrote many stories, plays, essays and broadcast scripts into which he introduced Gower characters and incidents—actual, partly-real and some wholly imaginary—with artistry, truth and affection. But in this book he was at great pains to efface himself, except for the task of selecting the material; and he succeeded in not interposing his own vision, however valid or perceptive, between the reader and the Gower people. Having gleaned from them, with the art that conceals art and eschews artifice, their own stories more fully and more articulately than perhaps many of them ever supposed they could have managed on their own, he has let them speak for themselves and their community. He has shown, once more, all his old consummate skill as a drama producer by encouraging these folk to be completely, naturally and unself-consciously themselves. And how eloquently and memorably they record their memories in their own distinctive words and turns of phrase; these instinctively individual, self-reliant, intelligent, gritty men and women of westernmost Gower, mostly, though not entirely of an earlier generation. Theirs was a frugal, Spartan, hard-working, isolated society before 1920, with little of the education and none of the luxuries now taken for granted; a community that has changed more in the last eighty years than in the 500 years beforehand. Then, as one of them rightly says in these pages, "people had to be quick and agile to get by''. In this book, thanks to Mansel's endless skill and patience and devotion, we can hear them talk with the untutored realism, ironic jocularity and down-to-earth good sense of plain men and women, who have often fought hard battles with poverty and adversity but rarely allowed themselves to be daunted or beaten. Their tale, like that of all earlier rural communities, is unique and is alive with the unheralded poetry and dignity of ordinary men and women's struggle for existence. In her splendid determination to see this book published, Mansel's wife, Gwen, worthily commemorates them and rescues their story from what might well have been perpetual oblivion. It is also, however, a fitting tribute to Mansel, who would have wished for no worthier memorial than his own faithful and undistorted mirror of a community of people whom he loved, with whom he identified and in whose midst he lived for so long.

Glanmor Williams

University College Swansea

About this Book

A few words are called for to explain the form which this volume has taken.

Gower has been a part of my life since I was two years old and I feel glad that I introduced it to Mansel because his sense of history and his immediate interest in the lives of Gower folk enabled him to see with fresh eyes many things which I took for granted. It became an ambition of his, which he did not live to see fulfilled, to compile an oral history of the western part of the peninsula, from the turn of the century until today, and in preparation for this he recorded conversations with many people who had lived their lives in the area.

The value of spoken history lies not so much in the discovery of new material as in the new perspective it gives to facts we already know. People who are still living act as bridges to the past, and the continuity in the lives of these people will be difficult for future generations to imagine if nothing is done to preserve their recollections. Of course, no one's memory is infallible, but it seems probable that oral history is closer to the truth than is official history.

Since Mansel's death, in February 1979, I felt compelled to see that the work he put into the project was not wasted, but I had no clear idea how he intended to present it—I think perhaps he would have combined the real characters into members of a hypothetical, cliff-top village. However, I decided on a different layout and have chosen to leave each person in his or her own locality—grouped under five broad headings.

Readers will quickly recognise cross-references to certain characters, occasions and customs, and I hope that, seen from different viewpoints, these will help to unify the picture in your mind. Again, in the extent of cutting, and in the finding of suitable illustrations, I have had to be guided by my instinct for what Mansel himself would have wanted.

We had been living in Rhossili ever since our marriage in 1939, and both our children were born and had their early education here. So although originally only 'Gower' by adoption, our roots are penetrating more deeply into the soil of this lovely place. For these reasons I am glad to be involved in bringing you this book, and hope it will add to your understanding and enjoyment of Gower.

Gwendolen Thomas

Rhossili 1982

Photographs

PART I

Roads
and Transport

WILL HARRY

Traction Engine Owner
Born at Cilibion 1886

'Today, unfortunately, traction engines are no longer to be seen travelling the roads of Gower. Gone are the days when you could walk along the top of Cefn Bryn on fine clear days and see the engines threshing and working all over the countryside. Gone are the days when you could see the smoke flying to the skies, and hear the shrill whistles of the engines echoing over the fields of Gower. No more will we hear the steady roaring of a threshing machine, nor see the traction engines jogging along with loads of from seven to twenty tons behind, along the un-surfaced narrow roads. Now, of course, everything is sacrificed to the great gods, the petrol and diesel engines. But consider the cost of running a steam engine as compared with that of a tractor. A steam engine will run happily on free sticks and water . . .!'

I was always mad on traction engines, from a very early age, and it was always an ambition of mine to be a traction engine owner. My father farmed Cilibion Farm, and I remember he had in his barn an old threshing machine with a steam engine to drive it. These must have been the first in these parts, I should think. They had belonged to a farmer called George Gower, from Norfolk, who turned out to be a very progressive fellow, and I heard him spoken highly of. One feat I heard tell of was his bringing eight brood mares together with stallions and colts by boat from Norfolk to Oxwich Bay! This was back in the 1850s. Anyway, he'd installed these machines in the barn, they were pretty clumsy things, mind, but on wet days you could see about twenty of the men, women and boys getting on with the threshing. It was an unusual sight, that, because before this, two men would spend every day the whole year round winnowing and threshing the corn with a flail or a threshel.

When I was a boy I drove Gower's threshing machine for my father. I was no older than five when he used to stand me on an oil drum to start the machine by turning a wheel, to let

'Threshing, new style'.

steam pass from the boiler to the engine . . . What appealed to
me was the general utility of a steam engine. We could thresh
with it, we could haul, uproot trees, plough, we could even pull
this house down. We could. With a threequarter-inch steel
rope. I have shifted boilers of 40 tons about the collieries. I'm
not very keen on oil, I like steam. I used to work horses too but I
never had any special delight in them.

    The time come now, when I was eighteen, my father decided
I should have a traction engine of my own. So one beautiful day
in 1906 a Mr Robinson, a representative from the Fowler traction engine builders of Leeds, drove up in a hansom cab, and
right into our hayfield. I was pitching the second crop of clover
hay in our 16 acre. He brought out catalogues, and he advised us
that for threshing work the most suitable type was the 6 N.H.P.
engine, you could handle it well in small yards . . . The upshot
of this visit was that we agreed to put in an order, and I heard
that I was invited to go up to Leeds for a while to visit the Fowler
workshops and learn the mechanical side of the engine world.
''We're giving you a chance we don't give others'', Mr Robin-

son told me. ''You'll learn more in a week than in a lifetime elsewhere''. And that turned out to be quite true. I was there for five or six weeks and saw every part of my machine being built and assembled. All that had to be done when I come home was the painting. A week later my engine was standing in a truck at Gowerton station! A mechanic from Fowler's stayed with us for two weeks afterwards to show me the proper driving of my steam engine, which I'd named *Dauntless*.

From that time I became a proper mechanic, a self-made one perhaps, but say something breaks inside, I can pull the whole engine down and put it all back again.

There was an interesting sequel to this, you know, a very long time after. In 1970, in June, I got an invitation from Fowler's to pay a return visit to their works. Sixty-four years since the first one!

'At the station in Leeds I was met by a car from Fowler's. I thought this was a very kind gesture on the part of the company. At the works I met numerous officials and the managing director. He was very interested to see the site where *Dauntless* was built all those years ago. I described to him what I had seen as a pupil, when they were building over twenty traction engines at a time. In those days the German government was one of their biggest customers, and Fowler's engines were used to draw many German guns through Belgium. I didn't notice a great deal of change about the place, except that, unfortunately, they were building now large caterpillar tractors instead. Everywhere I went they were very kind to me, though of the men that were working there 64 years ago, it was sad to see that not one remained.'

I found them all very comfortable people. They were all proper mechanics, you see, men who had been there from their teens, with more skill than anyone from the foundries. Yes, I found the Yorkshire people very open and friendly, I must say. Funnily enough, there was a coach from Yorkshire stopped outside our gate here the other day. They were touring, it seems. A charabanc. And the driver, he was only a boy really, we got talking, and he was very interested to hear about my trips to Leeds. Very comfortable chap he was, too.

I could have stayed at Fowler's and become a mechanic myself. I had the gift, you see. But I always had the ambition to be a businessman, and I'd sooner be on my own any day. So that's what happened really. I bought engine after engine, and for years I was managing six engines. And I had twelve men working for me. No need for that, I know, but I was ambitious, you see, I tackled things. I'm sorry to say that in the late 50s, on the advice of many farmers who told me that steam was on the way out, I broke up many of my proud engines. Since that time, of course, they have made a come-back especially among collectors, and now a good steam engine may change hands for several thousand pounds. There were two for sale in Cornwall the other day and I had the offer of them. One was £9,000, the other £8,000.

I made a lot of money in my time, but it went out again in buying engines. And say you invested £10,000 in threshing tackle, there was no compensation for taking work away from us. When tractors come in, I mean, farmers bought their own tackle, didn't want us any more . . . we had no security at all.

I delighted in the noise of the old steam engine. It never troubled me. Of course speed and time didn't matter much. We had solid tyres of course, there's no grip with rubber. With 20 tons behind you the wheels would slip on tarmac. We liked the stony roads. Full out, we could do six miles an hour. There were three-speed tractions and two-speed. On the hill the two-speed would do it fine but the three-speed was faster on the flat. When we were hauling—we did a tremendous amount of hauling during the First World War,—we would sometimes have two or three trucks behind. They could carry sixteen tons each, but we weren't supposed to carry more than eight tons in each, because of the weight on the roadway. Lorries didn't come to Gower till after 1920, so apart from the few buses we had the roads to ourselves. We filled the road completely . . .

'From 1880 to 1920 most of the haulage in Gower was done by two other traction engine owners, Greening of Killay and Gordon of Llanrhidian. For forty years they shifted thousands of tons of building materials for houses and farms. Bricks were brought from Killay and Swansea and sand from Oxwich Bur-

Road gang and steam roller.

rows. Greening's first engine arrived about 1879, and while it was still new, an amusing (or not so amusing!) incident happened whilst it was crossing Fairwood Common with a load. Across the common in the opposite direction came a smart carriage drawn by two proud horses. In the carriage sat Thomas Penrice, of Kilvrough Manor. The horses, taking fright at the oncoming monster, bolted and galloped away over the turf, tipping the carriage over and depositing the unfortunate gentleman on the indifferent ground! Partly as a result of this accident the local council decided in 1880 to forbid the movement of traction engines along the roads in day-time. If by chance this was unavoidable, some unfortunate chap was forced to walk in front carrying a red flag. These ridiculous bye-laws caused a large amount of discontent, but they were rigorously enforced for nearly twenty years. The National Traction Engine Owners Association eventually managed to get them repealed. This was not done without a fight, for in 1904 the county council was pressing to prevent traction engines working at all. Fortunately a Royal Commission was set up and its verdict was the roads were in fact for the use of, and should be constructed to suit, the traction engine . . .'

All this was just before my time, of course, but in my early years, before the First War, I spent a lot of time in hauling all manner of things: artificial manure from the Vivians' works at Hafod to the farms in Gower—at 5/- a ton; farm produce into Swansea; lime from the lime kilns—7/6 a ton. Hay, two or three wagons full, to the hay merchants in the town. We used to plan these trips so as to arrive in Swansea about midnight. We would then unload the hay, often helped by policemen, who enjoyed sharing the five gallon drum of beer left out for us by the hay-merchants. Building materials as well, of course. The first houses built at Mayhill, Swansea, were built from bricks hauled by me, as my engines were the only ones to tackle the hills. Furniture, too, we hauled. This was known for obvious reasons as "furniture bumping". On one memorable day we hauled behind one engine two furniture vans from Mumbles to Dowlais, over seventy miles. Heavy machinery and big boilers were often moved between collieries, up to twenty or thirty tons, no real difficulty. And coal, of course, that was a usual load, 6d a hundredweight. The bigger houses would take ten or twelve tons to last them a year. Penrice Castle was always a good customer of mine. They used 30 tons of coal a month to keep the big house in fires and to heat the greenhouses! The King Arthur would take ten tons, that would last them about four months. It was no job for an idler I can tell you. Sometimes we had to work day and night to master the job. I've been hauling thirty-six hours, look, without a break. Handling heavy loads two days and two nights. I didn't mind it. I must have been tough when I was younger.

The engine would burn coal of course, but if there was a shortage, say during the General Strike, we could keep going easily on sticks. Only thing, it takes such a lot of wood to keep going.

Then there was the threshing. There were several threshing machines to be seen around Gower in the 1880s and 90s. My first was bought in 1905, and there was plenty of work for her right away. Sometimes thirty or forty farmers would want the machines at the same time. We'd need a few days at each place usually. Say we went down to Rhossili or Pitton. We'd warn the farmer we were coming, because it was the custom then to stop on the job. He knew he'd have to put up two men for the night, and it worked well. He'd kill a sheep or a pig in readiness, and we fed really well. Specially prepared. I was single then, so I would work on sometimes till it got dark. For most men it was a day's outing. The farmer would brew some beer or get in a cask, and there was a fair amount drunk. Beer was good for swilling the dust down you see. A lot of fellows couldn't stand the dust, many had to pack up in middle age, with dust, or fog, on the lungs. Not a lot of wheat grown, mostly oats and barley. Compared with the combine harvester, the traction engine outfit was able to clean it better. It had a much bigger area to riddle it. And a traction engine would last you a lifetime.

There was more fun to the job then. We used to chat around the fire in the evening, or sometimes, if there'd been plenty of beer flying, we'd have a bit of a concert. Men would come from other farms, and start up a dance. That used to happen even more in the days when we used to cut and tie the corn by hand. Then it was a real Reapers' Feast like you hear about from ancient times, it goes back to the Bible, doesn't it . . . the feast for the reapers. There was a custom then for everyone to tie a band round the last sheaf in the field, but it died out when I was young . . . What caused a lot of nasty feeling in Gower was when the Government did tax the farmers if they brewed their own beer. Fool of a thing really, they had to have a licence! The farmers didn't pay much attention to it, as far as I was aware, but it left a nasty feeling all the same.

For sixty-four years I've done forest sawing and timber hauling all over South Wales. My tools for this job were my steam traction engines and portable rack saw-benches, taking saws of up to six foot in diameter and capable of dealing with logs on the site of up to twenty feet in length.

'I remember buying my last portable rack saw-bench. It was during the Second World War and we were laden with so much work that I found the need for another bench. I applied to the Forestry Commissioners at Cardiff for a permit, but they were unable to grant me one. I asked the forestry people in Bristol; again I was turned down. I decided to go to London to apply to the head office of the Tools Commission. People told me I was foolish to try, but I set out for London, undaunted. I found the offices, next door to the War Office. At the door a porter asked me my business. I told him, then I was introduced to an officer higher up the scale who told me, if I would wait two hours, he could introduce me to the head of the Tools Commission! Sure enough, two hours later I was led into a large comfortable office where I met him, he was a kind-looking old gentleman with flowing white hair. He told me to make myself comfortable and explain what I wanted . . . I found him a pleasant man to talk to and we chatted comfortably for some time about various topics. He ended the interview by writing out a permit for me to buy a portable rack saw-bench. This I did, for I was told by the gentleman that there was one for sale at Dunster Castle in Somerset . . .'

We used to work deep in the woods, the engines being fed on refuse from the branches . . . we also did some jobs extracting

large trees from deep ravines, a job most other people wouldn't tackle. I have extracted some of the biggest oaks in Wales from a terrifyingly steep ravine at the foot of the Black Mountains, in the Llandybïe area. We had to wind the enormous logs with two engines up a steep incline of nearly 200 yards. It took us two and a half years.

During the First War, in Gower, two woods were cut down, the 170 acre Cilibion Wood and the Decoy Wood, which was about 25 acre, and I hauled the timber away from there. Incidentally, the Cilibion Wood has grown up again now fully! I did a lot of this work for Lord Swansea, he was one of my best customers. He was always full of ideas, and it was he who had set up this Decoy Wood, with the Decoy Pool in it. This was a pond, about the size of Broad Pool, which he had constructed. It had reeds all round it higher than a man's head. It was a copy of one that Lord Amherst had on his Norfolk estate, I understand. He kept up to a dozen tame ducks permanently on the pond and this attracted wild fowl flying across from Llanrhidian marshes and Oxwich and such places. They would hear the tame ducks quacking on the water, and if you took a peep during the winter months, especially when it was frosty, you would see hundreds of wild ducks and geese on the pond. There were three little channels made up of girders and covered over with nets and these led out of the pond, you see, and the ducks would get trapped in these channels, sort of trap door arrangement, the net would be as big as this room. Very successful it was, I remember the keepers coming up through our yard with a load of ducks, as much as they could carry. No trace of the Decoy Pool now of course.

Another idea Lord Swansea had was his chemical works. You see, a lot of timber was being left to rot in the Parc-le-Breos Woods and Cilibion, and he said couldn't nothing be done with it? He hated waste, but no one would take the trouble to haul it away. So he built the Llethrid Chemical Works in the Cilibion Woods, at the end of the last century that would be. And he got a big waggoner wearing white fustian clothes to collect up the waste timber, with a gambo and two horses. And he took these boughs and things to the coke-ovens he had built, and these turned them into charcoal, lumps the size of eggs. This charcoal was used then in his copper works at Hafod in the refining processes. And the juice and the sap, which was known as naphtha, was sold for the manufacture of medicines. He was a good businessman, was Lord Swansea. He had ambition, you see; after his day there wasn't the go in the Hafod that there was when he was alive. When he died the Hafod died.

I was talking to an old man who had worked with Lord Swansea for years. He was telling me of a typical incident when he lived at Singleton, which he built of course out of his profits from copper—trading with all the nations of the world. Anyway, bad news come to Singleton. He was having dinner, big piece of beef on the table, and the word come that the men at the works had gone on strike. He caught hold of the beef and slinged it across the room in his temper. He got his coachman to get his horse ready, and then he drove up to Hafod full trot. The men were all waiting at the entrance. He jumped off his horse, told one of the men to hold it, and he made a speech to them on the spot. He offered to show them the books to prove that the dividends were down, to 5% or something, and he couldn't see his way to paying them any more money. And he told them to go back to work, otherwise, he said, he would pack the works up, it would be more economical for him he said, to move the works to Germany. Instead of having to cross the North Sea he would be able to get his stuff more easily to Denmark and Russia. "You please yourselves," he said, "you can lie down, all of you, but if you do, I'll be off, it'll pay me better". They saw his point, and went back to work. There was something in his head, you see, he wasn't dull, was he?

JOSEPH JOHN HOSKINS

Horse-bus and General Haulage driver
Born in Llanmadoc 1894

They tell me I hold a bit of a record, with the horse-buses, like. I started with one horse then later we used two, and before I finished I'd be driving a team of three, to carry a heavy load—for market in summer, say. Prince, Bright and Darling, they were the boys. Darling out in front—he was a good leader. Not easy to get a horse to take the lead, mind. But they'd know every inch of the way. It was my father started, a long time ago. Oh, before I was born. Him and my grandfather did a lot of haulage. One thing, they had a little barge, that'd carry a load up to thirty tons. They'd keep it in Cheriton Pill, and take limestone across to Llanelli, it was specially quarried stone for to do some job over in the works there. And they'd bring back a load of general cargo, coal mostly. Then people would come from all over Gower with their donkeys and horse and cart to buy it.

My father used to do a lot of haulage of stone for the roads and things, so to help people take their stuff into Swansea Market he started a horse-bus, pretty little thing it was, made by

Horse-bus at Llanmadog, pre 1912.

Jackett's in Swansea. We had a wagonette as well, and I started
driving that before I left school. I think I was twelve, and my
mother used to come after me to help. We might get a telegram
asking us to meet some people arriving at Llanmorlais station,
coming on their holidays, maybe. My father was doing the
horse-bus, so I'd drive the wagonette. When I was about fifteen I
took over the horse-bus. It was a hard job, harder for the horses.
The roads were shockers. Wheels were all solid. Lighting just
candles, of course. We always carried a hammer in case a three-
cornered stone got stuck in the frog of the horse's hoof. You
might see him go lame, so you'd stop and knock it out. Always
the same route: from Llanmadoc to Cheriton, through Old
Walls, always stop at The Greyhound—the old people used to
call it The Dog—then Cilibion, Fairwood Common to Killay.
And another thing, if there was any frost about, my father had a
special kind of nail that he'd fix on the horse's foot, to stop him
slipping. He could go up the side of a house with them in. My
father was very clever with that sort of thing. I never became an
expert.

The farmers around used to breed the right type of horse for the job—big body, good bones, good feet and wind—but before we took one it'd have to pass the vet.

Mind you we had to work hard in those days, or starve. But it gave us quite a good living. There was a licence to pay, of course, and if one of the horses failed, it'd cost us thirty or forty pounds to replace him. But we done all right. No shortage of passengers one way or the other. And we'd do quite a business in orders for people. We'd put it all down in our book, then they'd pay us on our return home. We went to the same shops mostly and got a little commission for the business we brought. 3d or 6d then for doing the message. Some of the farmers never bothered to pay every time. They'd have an account with us, and we'd send them a bill every month. I enjoyed my life on the road. You'd get to know everybody and all their business. Of course, the horse-buses finished about 1912, when the motor-bus came in. I was only nineteen then, so it wasn't long before I was with them. And I must say I liked them even better. The horses were slow going, mind. With the motor-bus you did more trips and saw more places. I worked as a conductor for a

First motor bus—a Pioneer outside Culverhouse, Porteynon, *ca.* 1912.

while, and then as a driver. And all my life after that, for the next forty years. In the early days the money was good, mind. Eight bob a day for conducting, ten bob for driving, with 15/- on Saturdays and 12/6 on Sundays. That would be after the First War, about 1920.

That was my life, and I was always happy with it.

JIM BROCKIE

Bus Driver

Born at Sanctuary Farm 1897

My mother used to say: "Tie him to a horse's tail, and he's landed". I didn't want anything else, I was just passionately interested in horses, riding them and working them . . . any donkey or pony that happened to be strolling around—cockler's donkeys of course, we used to catch them and ride them about —we always dabbled with horses when we were kids. And I got quite a dab hand at breaking them in. We'd never ill-treat them, mind, not like they do today,—youngsters catch ponies these days and drive them till they drop. Murderous I call that.

Then I went to work in the stables for my uncle, at Bovehill. He had seven horses, and I was what the Breconshire boys called the 'lumper', the helper in the stable. At half past five in the morning my uncle used to rattle the door and get us out. He reckoned we should do eight hours in the field every day. We'd be out by eight, unhook at 12, dinner, then hook up at 2, and finish at 6. I say finish, but you had to clean and groom the horses after that, and bed them down. It was a full day. My uncle used to go round the stables at night-time and if he felt a bit of a sweat-mark around the collar, on the breasts or on their shoulders, he'd play holy pop. "A horse is like you", he'd say, "he likes to be clean and comfortable before he goes to bed, remember that." . . . of course, these days, all the farm worker has to do is jump off the tractor and shove it in the shed, and that's that for the day. We used to care for a horse. Very few youngsters round today who could put a collar on.

In my Army days then, I started as a gunner but ended up as a shoeing smith. I was on the Somme, at Ypres, and Lille, with an ammunition column of mules. I had fifty mules to look after on my own. Mind you, a bad mule is much more difficult than a bad horse. Simple to shoe when they're quiet, because there's more depth of wall on a mule's foot than there is on a horse's. They can be difficult to shoe, and handle. But a good team of mules is very tough, it would kill a team of horses, easy. Some of them were never out of action for weeks on end, but they didn't seem to take any notice of shell-fire; as long as their drivers were there with them, you see; there'd be this relationship.

When I came home from the Army, my younger brother was very keen on starting a bus service, from Old Walls to Swansea. Horse-buses as such had finished then of course. Anyway, our funds didn't run to a bus, so we settled for a lorry, and for a year or two did some hauling. Then in 1920, George Taylor of Vanguard Motors formed a new company, the Vanguard Motors (1920) Ltd. He asked my mother to put some money into the firm, and she told him: "I'll put the lorry in, on condition that Will and Jim get a job with the company." So that's what started me off as a bus driver. From Rhossili. I went there in 1920 and never left. I used to take a bus in on Mondays, Wednesdays, Fridays and Saturdays, one bus a day, leaving about 7.30 in the morning and returning about five. I enjoyed every minute of my bus life, though in those early days there was a wet shirt for me by the time we loaded up everything in the morning. We carried everything and everybody—this was part of the service we gave, not an occasional favour for people. There'd be a charge, a bob perhaps for bringing a live calf down! Same with parcels of groceries—coming home, the top of the bus would be piled up with groceries. On the way in perhaps I'd have to pull in at Tucker's Pitton Cross and pick up a pig split down the middle, to deliver it to a pork butcher's in Wind Street. Then we'd have to go round the builders' merchants and pick up timber and cement and things, and that would have to be delivered that night.

The roads were twisting and turning and all limestone, of course, full of potholes. You could always see a bus coming miles away, by the clouds of dust rising above it. Horse-brakes were about the only other traffic then, bringing parties out a few miles from town on a summer outing. The old bus would have acetylene lamps and solid tyres, and the brakes were just metal to metal, the footbrake was on the shaft, not on the wheels, and the drum was set just behind the gearbox, so if your side-shaft went, your brake was useless. I drove the first Gardiner diesel that came to Swansea, about 1927. But the first engines we had were Dennises, then Thorneycroft, Tilling-Stephens, and the first double-decker was a Leyland. We had a Gardiner engine fitted into a Tilling-Stephens chassis—the Rolls Royce of diesels the Gardiner was. The Dennis 40 h.p. was all right, but not a lot of power in it. The engines were always governed though, of course, 12 m.p.h. was the most we were allowed. We did tie up the governer sometimes—out of sight out of mind! But the roads were so rough you couldn't open up too much. You can imagine

Vanguard bus, 1920.

Jim Brockie, driver (centre right) and Morgan Gibbs, conductor (centre left),
outside Shepherd's, Parkmill, 1922.

the bumping we used to get anyway, with just the four springs
to take it. We very often smashed the front springs in the potholes. When you think of the way they used to make the roads
then: the roadmen would be cracking piles of loose stones at the
roadside, they'd put a layer of these on the roadway, then a layer
of dirt or mud, the roller would go over it, with a water tank,
and there'd just be a heap of mud left, like cement. Before long
the suction of a wheel would pull out a stone, and very soon
there'd be a pothole. And then mud, and dust in the summer,
the conductor would spend most of his time in the summer
walking around with a duster, cleaning the seats. It would swirl
in through the back—but I was driving, I'd be all right! . . . Non-
bus days were given to servicing the vehicle and cleaning her
up. Of course you didn't have the feeling for the engine as you
used to have for horses. But I used to love the old bus. I really
cared for it. And if I bumped it or even got a scratch, I'd break
my heart. These days, I don't know . . . most drivers wouldn't
worry if half the side of their bus got ripped away!

There was a time when we used to carry a tremendous load of people, in summer-time. I've seen queues in Rhossili waiting to go back to town, oh, more than a hundred yards long, and we'd be going as hard as ever we could to clear them back, with three buses. Until they put a stop to it, we used to carry them hanging on anywhere, even on the luggage roof. I remember old Sgt Thorne, the Inspector in Swansea,—he would be prowling around in the mornings to see if we had anyone on top, but some got wise to this and would run to the next stop and climb up there. Interesting life, mind you, you got to know everyone. For a while it used to be like the days of the horse-bus. In fact, old Will Vernal (Fernhill) who used to drive the horse-bus, would always jump in and sit in the front with me, and every person we'd meet on the road, he'd want to know who it was. If I couldn't tell him, he'd say: "Well, boy, thee's ought to know; —I did . . ." We'd stop anywhere in those days, for anybody, no official bus stop anywhere in those days. Bus drivers today will as soon drive past you as pick you up. They don't seem interested in the job, or the service to the public. They're just there to fill a gap. They dress any old how. I had to wear a uniform, white collar, white shirt, black tie, almost regimental. We had very good hours and we were keen. John Watts was our man, it was he bought up the smaller companies to form the United Welsh.

Driving the bus was as good a job as you could get. I was paid by the day, came to about £5 a week, that was a very good wage. And there was this tradition of public service, of helping people. The first thing I used to do when I stopped was jump out of the cab and give a hand to anyone struggling with luggage. How much of that do you see today? Eventually of course I was on the road every day of the week, and some people, I remember, wouldn't make the journey into town unless I was driving the bus! And for a long time the people of Gower were considered in, say—the making out of a new timetable. George Taylor used to ask us, now do you think these times would suit so-and-so, or so-and-so—people who we knew relied on the bus service at fixed times. Now of course the public has to fall in with anything the firm decides.

Then came the operation on my leg. I did get frost-bite in my left leg in the First World War, that might have been the cause, but I smoked too much, too, I was guilty there. Anyway, I got a blockage, my left leg turned septic, gangrene set in, and I had to have it amputated. What price my driving career now, I thought. "What's your intention?" the doctor asked me after taking my leg off. "Back to drive the bus", I said, "one day". "Good for you", he said, "there's no reason why you shouldn't". When I saw the traffic manager, he came over with the rough stuff . . . "Well, you either can or you can't", he said to me in the end. "I'll prove to you that I can", I said. He rattled me a bit, mind, but others were helpful.

I was disapppointed for another reason too—that I would never do any farming now, when I retired. Because all my life farming has been my main interest, even when I was in the bus. When I'd take a party on a Mystery Tour, I had the reputation of dawdling along quietly, looking about me to see what this farmer was doing or that one, enjoying every moment of the trip, and people used to come to me afterwards and say "Thank you, driver, for not driving too fast, we've had time to look around for a change and enjoy the countryside . . ."

Still, driving was different—easier than walking—and I was determined. Like I used to be with horses. Very funny creatures. You've got to make up your mind that you're going to beat that animal, or he'll beat you, then you've had it. And he's finished for everybody. If a horse has chucked you off once or twice he'll do it with anyone who comes near him. I felt the same about the bus and driving. So the first day I had my artificial leg I got in my car and drove it. And one of the boys came down to see me with a bus. "Jump in, Jim," he said, "see what you can do with it". I got in but I could not push the clutch out, I didn't have the strength. So I got a plank and fixed it in the shed so that if I put my back against the wall, the plank would give when I stepped on it. That's how I built up my muscles. And the next time I got into a bus, I had no difficulty in pushing the clutch out. And soon I was back driving normally again. Help yourself, I say, no one else will do it for you.

PART II

Some of the Older Inhabitants

ALICE TAYLOR

Postmistress

Born in Horton 1881

This house is about 300 years old now, it's always been our family house,—my father was born here, and his father . . . and I was born here, 94 years ago. My father was a boot and shoe maker. There was a very good trade in those days, because there wasn't much machinery. He got a machine to do the sewing, then the foreign shoes come in and he had to give it up, there wasn't much to make at it. In the last, I gave the machine to the old iron. That's him up there on the wall, and that's my mother, she died when she was 29. I've got reminders of the family all about me here. That old sword over the mantelpiece, for instance. Father's grandfather brought that home here—I'm not going to tell you all that blooming story, my father used to yarn about it so often that I swore I'd never talk about it again. Anyway, his grandfather was in a vessel travelling out with copper ore, to South America I should think, a bad place for hurricanes anyway. There was another vessel in distress and he went to rescue them. French soldiers on board it seems, officers. And one of the officers presented him with that great big thing. It used to shine like anything, but we got tired of polishing it, so we put Brunswick black all over it. A dress sword it is, never been used. Not yet, anyway!

We used to have a lot more fun in the village,—nothing much at all now. We knew everybody, what they was having for dinner and what they wasn't. But now I can't go into anybody's house, only one perhaps. The foreigners here now they don't know nothing about me . . . On a Saturday we used to go into Swansea on the horse-bus. I could only afford to go about once a month, it cost half-a-crown, they charged me two shillings because I was so small. Great fun it was, we had to get out and climb the hills of course. Father used to sell a few potatoes, but when the foreigners come in, he had to stop that. We'd get up at quarter to four,and we'd get to town by about half past nine. There's Tom Nicholas on that picture, he's taking the horses

Horton, *ca.* 1920.

down the hill from the bus, the bus house was near Bank Farm.
The horse in front is the colt.

And when I was a girl, I used to help with the visitors at the
big houses. There've been visitors at Horton since before my
time. They were a different class of people then, not the working classes as they are now. They were from Oxford, and places
like that,—from the colleges. They'd take one of the big houses
for a month. I remember in the First World War they were asked
to take them for three months, but that didn't work really.
Never had Welsh visitors at all. I don't think I've ever met any. I
wish I had really, I'd love to have learned Welsh. I think it's a
lovely language, sounds so homely somehow. But I could never
turn my tongue to it, I don't think.

I used to help with the rooms and the meals. My goodness, I
can remember when I got my first shilling at the Hollies! A shilling a week! I thought I was pretty rich then. They used to give
me all the soft jobs, but I looked after them well, and I loved it.
Somebody said I was just an ornament down there! They used
to hire a brake and go around on picnics, all their servants with
them. But people with children would stay near the beach, and
most of them would bathe. Us girls used to go bathing, too, on

the way home from school, with nothing on at all. Not a soul on the beach then. Imagine doing that now!

It wasn't long before I escaped from the village. I went into service, in Llandaff first, then in East Grinstead. Lovely big houses. Here to stay I thought. I nearly broke my heart when I had to come home. My mother had died, my sister had gone to stay in Oxford and wouldn't come home, so I had to come back and look after my father. He was the quietest man who ever lived, so there was no bother with him. But I had to leave—a lovely place, oh it was grand. About £20 a year but lots of fun. And they used to treat me really good, it seemed to me it was Sunday every day, after this place. But I had to come home. I wasn't going to stay long here, that was my idea. But that was sixty years ago, and here I am still. I was sad about it at first, but then a few years later I took over the village shop, with the Post Office. That was in 1919, and I had it for thirty-five years. The woman who'd kept the first-ever Post Office and shop in Horton, she'd died, and I took it over. I must have had cheek enough in those days, I couldn't do it now. At first I took the shop but not the Post Office. So we were without one for a while. I didn't want it, I didn't know anything about a Post Office. But Mr Turner the minister, he got tired of going to Porteynon for his penny stamp, so he went into Swansea and got the job for me, from the GPO—just to save he going to Porteynon! So I had to take the blooming thing. It was a small Post Office, no money orders, only stamps and pensions and things, but I was frightened to death at first. But then I got to love it,—it was really a very interesting job. I used to know everything that was going on in the village,—one would come and tell me a bit, then another would tell me a bit, but by the end of the day I'd know the lot!

It was then I was sorry though that I hadn't learned a bit more in school . . . we had quite a good teacher but the girls weren't given the chances the boys were. We had no geography at all. The boys used to go around with maps, but we learned nothing about geography, and that's what I like best now. Father was going to sea and he had schooling till he was eighteen but he never went in the end,—he had an illness. He taught me all I

know about maps and things, and when I get the inclination
now, I can keep looking at a map all day, finding different places
. . . I could have done with much more schooling, but there . . .
it might not have been a good thing for me in the end . . .

. . . If I'd gone away and never come back, my life would have
been very different, I suppose . . . I don't think I'd have got married, but I never bothered, I wasn't the marrying sort. I was very
delicate for one thing. Not much better now.

ARTHUR DAVIES

Carpenter
Born in Landimore 1884

I'll tell you something about Arthur's Stone. You know the big
flat piece lying at the side, as if it has split off? . . . Well, I can tell
you, David Jones of Stonemill cut that off. If you notice, there
are little hollows at the edge of the stone lying on the ground,
and they match some marks on the main stone up there, that's
where he put his borer, you see. That's a bar with a chisel end
that he'd be using. What he had in mind was to dress it and take
it for a millstone, but after he cut it off he found he couldn't do
anything with it, it was too heavy for him and he had to leave it
there. Father told me all about that, he knew the fellow who
done it. In my young days, a lot of strangers used to come down
and walk round Arthur's Stone with their books open. It didn't
mean much to the old people of the village, but some of them
used to say that King Arthur was travelling in the train through
Llanelli, and he found a pebble in his boot. He took it out and
threw it away and it landed on Cefn Bryn, and it grew there!

Another thing my father told me about was the Stouthall
Stone, that's the one standing in the centre of a pile of stones,
on the left of the Stouthall Road as you go from the village.
Good Lor, you should see the people there, with their papers all
out. "Dost thee know who's buried there, boy?" my father
asked me. "No," I said. "Well, 'tis only Colonel Wood's white

King Arthur Hotel, Reynoldston, 1923.

horse, the old charger what he used to follow the hounds with''. You see, they kept deers at Stouthall then, and they'd take these out to Rhossili Down and the Colonel would lead a hunt there after the hounds. And I remember seeing the hooks in the wall of the Stouthall barn where they used to fasten the deers up to.

All the roads used to lead to Reynoldston. It was the centre village after all. It had the main Post Office and the mail would go out from here every morning. Postmen were all on foot then, bar the man at Porteynon,—he had a pony to ride, a trap later as well. Well he'd pick up the mail, go first to Penrice Castle, then down to Oxwich, across to Slade, through the fields to Horton Cross. Over the burrows then to Porteynon, then Overton, and he'd stable his pony up with old Sylvanus Bevan. Quite a trip, once a day. Me and another boy, we were thirteen then, we used to do it for a spell.

Reynoldston was where the fairs were held, too. The big one was Harvest Fair, September 17th. My Lor, that was a big day. Hundreds and hundreds of people came to that. A good fair, a beautiful fair it was. There was swings, of course, and side-shows and a boxing booth, but what sticks in my mind is the Wild Beast Show—I'm going back over eighty years now—that was something! They'd come down on a Sunday and two elephants would be pulling them. I remember once they missed Reynoldston and got lost on the Rhossili road. There was two of every animal, in cages inside a marquee, two bears, two lions, two tigers . . . I remember father taking me there when I was about seven, and there was a girl performing with a great big lion. She went into his cage at last, put a white cloth over her head, the old lion opened his mouth wide and she shoved her head right inside. Father seen me jump, see, and he said, "Don't thee tak' any notice, boy, she's well used to that".

There was always a beer tent as well, though the fair was held right outside the doors of the King Arthur. My father and mother used to keep The Three Brothers at Landimore—it's gone now—and they used to come over and look after this beer tent sometimes. Everything open all day then, of course, so there was a fair drop of beer drunk, I can tell you. The best beer was 2½d a pint, or you could get a 'pint of four', that would be two pints at 2d a pint. The working men would sink a dozen pints, and think nothing of it. I didn't touch beer myself till I was married, that'd be sixty-nine years ago. And I'll tell you the way I started. 'Twas very hot summer weather, and I came to my mother's to help with the bit of hay. The drink then, especially at harvest, was 'glaster'—that was milk and water mixed. Well, as I say, this tremendously hot day, me and my mother were turning the hay. And that evening I was bad. And mother said to me "What about a drop of glaster, boy?" "No, thanks," I said, "I had enough of that yesterday, I feel sick, I think the heat have curdled the milk". "Well, have a glass of beer, boy, that won't hurt you". So I did. And that was the first glass of beer I ever tasted. Made up for it since, mind. Though I can't get to the King now unless I get a lift.

A carpenter I am by trade, though I didn't settle back in the village until 1927. At eighteen I went away to Ebbw Vale to do my apprenticeship in joinery. No wages then for five years. Then at twenty-one you could qualify for the full tip for a journeyman, this was 7½d an hour. In Swansea it was 8½d an hour. Foreman got 9d or 9½d. I did a fifty-four hour week then for £1.18.3d, that was it. Good gosh, they don't know they're born today . . . When I come back to the village it was mostly repair work, not many new houses going up then. But I did a lot of work with the churches, and the rectories, for the Church Commission. I worked a bit with Parson Davies (J. D. Davies) at Llanrhidian. He was a clever fellow, did all the cornices and bosses himself. And very soon I became the village undertaker. I had promised way back that if anything happened to Will Lewis, I'd start. So when he went, so many came to ask me that I had to take it up. In those days, mind, we had to plane up the coffins ourselves, and you had to be very careful with the joint- ing, especially the bottoms,—they were liable to leak, you see. Now of course anyone can call himself an undertaker if he buys the whole thing ready, with all the fittings on. My gosh, I've buried a whole host of Gower people in my time, I suppose I've made over three hundred coffins altogether. I think I was one of the cheerful undertakers. Though I couldn't show it, of course. I mean, if you take it too gloomy, it can affect you badly. You've got to take your mood from the mourners, haven't you? And I could do that all right. It didn't cost so much to die then. A nice elm coffin would be about £9. A seven foot grave could be dug for 7/6—now it'll cost you 10 quid. 'Tisn't often you'd have a hearse. They'd mostly carry, you see. With all the family walk- ing behind, of course. Yes, miles and miles. And if possible, bury on a Sunday, when the men weren't at work. Very rare now to bury on a Saturday or a Sunday, if they can help it.

I haven't begun to think about death myself, yet. Well, I'm only ninety-two. Still, as one old fellow used to say to me: ''Ay, Arthur boy, time doth flow''.

I buried him, too.

LEWIS JOHN

Welsh Settler

Born at Ty'rcoed 1890

Our farm at Ty'rcoed was a bit of an oddity, really. We were a
Welsh family that had settled in English Gower,—only just
inside, mind. We were the furthest west of the Welsh farms, I
believe. But we had the best of both worlds, really, because my
grandfather, who spoke nothing but Welsh as a young man,
went and married the daughter of a Gower farmer. So the Gower
way of speaking was familiar to us. We knew it and I could
speak it as well as anybody, really. Only Father didn't like it,
and didn't allow us to talk in that way. You see, he was very
keen on education, he was a big public man locally and he was
governor of the Gowerton Intermediate School when it opened
in 1896, and he thought that the Gower dialect was un-
educated, like. He was keen on us speaking proper English.

But there were Gower words all about us—in the kitchen, for
instance. We had a very big kitchen, with a table to seat twelve
to fourteen at a time, it was flagged and sprinkled with sand. I
used to fetch this in a horse and trap from Cwm Ivy burrows.
One house near us had a trodden earth floor, also sprinkled with
sand. Beams, of course, with hooks, huge dresser, settles and
cupboard bed to one side of the hearth. On the other side was
the pentan (hob). It was a vast fireplace, and more light came
into the room through that than by the windows. You could see
the stars if you looked up inside. There was a large oak beam
supporting the inner wall of the chimney, massive thing it was,
and that was called the clevvy place. And above that was the
charnel, where you kept hams and things, that was a box-like
structure going up above the ceiling. Lighting was by tallow
candles—though when I was young the butcher used to make
candles, out of mutton fat, with some string for the wick. We
used a big brick oven for baking bread, it was in a back kitchen. I
don't know how she did it, but my mother always managed to
bake it perfectly, never over done. She'd cook dowset in it too.
That was like what we'd call custard tart, only it was about four

inches thick. In winter we'd have shickan for breakfast. A sort of thick porridge. I remember my grandmother used to spend nearly an hour making that, sprinkling oatmeal bit by bit into a pan of boiling water. We'd have a couple of basins of that on the table, with a basin of milk for us to dip in and help ourselves. Then on sheep-washing days, in June, she used to make cheese cakes,—these were made from curd, with the pastry like a turn-over. We often made our cheese from sheep's milk. My word, the women worked very hard in those days. The farmer's wife, you see, would pay for the groceries from what she could get by selling butter and eggs and poultry. My mother used to send twenty pounds of butter every week to Swansea market.

I liked farming very much and I was sorry in a way I went for a job in Swansea when I was eighteen. But my elder brother kept on, and my father wanted me to 'get on'. Of course the war came, and that was that. I had three and half years in Palestine. When I came back my father wanted me to go back to Ty'rcoed, but I was twenty-nine then, and really I had got out of touch, I had lost the value of animals. But I was a terror for work as a boy, and what the Gower people called vitty-handed, I could turn my hand to most jobs. Even when I was twelve I used to keep up with the men scything the corn. That was a hard job, you had to catch the corn in the crooks on the scythe, the zive as we called it, turn round and lay it down like a little swathe. We'd bind it after with some of the corn itself. I remember well the wonder we felt at the first mechanical reaper and binder we saw.

My pocket money then came from rabbits. A couple of us boys used to spend a lot of time coursing rabbits in the fields—the ones from our neighbours' fields always seemed better than our own, so we risked being chased. Though when they found out we weren't those poachers from Penclawdd, all was well. We would send the rabbits we caught into Swansea by John Rees's horse-bus, from Llangennith, he'd sell them for us, give us 7d each and keep 3d, his commission. If we had a hare to sell, of course, that was a small fortune, about half-a-crown. Rabbits were used for barter, too. If you could catch him sober, the postman used to cut our hair for us. Payment, one rabbit.

But that horse-bus was a sight! Nothing to see sheep on board, with their legs tied, or a calf's head sticking out of a sack, or hear a cockerel crowing from a basket.

I also had the job of walking the cattle to the butchers. Ours were pretty well-fed, fat ones, so I had a job of keeping them from sitting down; that would have been the end. But Mr Brown the butcher always said that ours were as good a sample of cattle as he had seen in the west of Glamorgan. We'd get about 10/6 a score for them, deadweight.

Looking back now, over seventy years, everyone seems to have been so friendly, and cheerful, in those days. I never heard anyone addressed as Mister, for instance. It was Sam o'Leason, Will o'Vernal, and that. There was a story of a man coming down from Swansea, to Burry Green. He stopped a local and asked him : "Excuse me, can you tell me where Mr Taylor lives round here?" "Mr Taylor?" the fellow replied, "I don't know no Mr Taylor living here", he said, "but there's a Rawley Taylor in that house across the road". Then there were some great get-togethers. Like the chapel anniversary at Old Walls. This was always held in June, and we'd make sure all our walls were white-washed before that. The chapel would be packed, benches from the Greyhound that had held drunks the night before would be put in the aisles, the preachers were full of "hwyl", and we used to have at least sixteen to tea at Ty'rcoed, round our big kitchen table. Another great day was Reynoldston Fair—17th of September. One boy I knew, he was dying to go to the fair, but the farmer decided to hoe the swede rows, and keep the boy to lead the horses. At the end of one row the boy turned to the farmer and said, "Hey, maister, art bad? Thee's not looking too well". "I'm all right, boy", the farmer said, doubtfully. A few more turns, and the boy tries again. Eventually his master starts to believe he was poorly, so he gives up the job for the day, and the boy got to the fair, with its coconuts, and its boxing and the lady's teasers—heaven knows what the health authorities of today would have had to say about them!

The first school I went to was at Llanrhidian, about one and a half miles to walk. If we were lucky we might get a ride in a coal cart. But there was one objectionable coalman, Will One-Eye.

He would never let us climb on, he'd make us run behind the cart all the way. Then he'd say sometimes: "Art tired, boy?" "Ay, I am that", I'd reply. "Well now, if thee's ha' axed me for a ride, thee coos't a had 'n, but there thee's lowst it!" And he'd just laugh at us.

When I was twelve, in 1902. I went to the Gowerton Intermediate. We had to pay £1 3s 8d a year. I was the first one to go from our part of Gower, so it was quite a thing. I had to lodge during the week of course, I stayed with an aunt of my father's. So on Monday morning I caught the 8.30 train from Llanmorlais for Gowerton. I had to do a job of work every morning before setting out, clean out the cowsheds or something. Then I'd leave the house at about a quarter to eight, with a carpet bag filled with grub and clothes and schoolbooks, perhaps a plate of tart my mother had made, or half a dozen eggs. But I used to travel to the station in style. To save me walking the couple of miles with that load, I used to go to a field next to the house, and catch our pony, Doll, wonderful pony she was. I got on her bare back, no saddle or bridle, just a bit of a twig to guide her. And we'd set off for Llanmorlais. I had no trouble with Doll at all.

Gowerton train at Penclawdd station, 1912.

She was inclined to be frightened of the cocklers' donkeys if we
met any, and as our way lay along the morfa, the old marsh road
under Cil Ifor, the estuary and the sea to our left, we did have to
watch the tide. Sometimes at high tides, Doll, who was only fifteen hands high, had to almost swim through the seawater that
had filled up there. Father was nearly drowned there once. Anyway, once at the entrance to Station Road, Doll and I parted
company. I gave her a pat on the back and turned her home-
wards. By mid morning the folk at home would be expecting to
see her at the gate, waiting for someone to open it for her. She
got so used to this freedom that she could never be persuaded to
get into shafts and pull a trap.

Come Friday evening, lessons finished at 4.30 in those days, I'd call at my aunt's for a cup of tea, collect my empty carpet bag and a school bag of books for my weekend homework, then I'd walk home, always, all the way, rain or shine, and I'd take a route cross country, about eight miles, pleasant walk in the summer, but in winter it was often dark before I set out, and a lot of the way was over fields and cart tracks, up to my ankles in mud sometimes, and under those clumps of trees it was as dark as a bag . . . I usually looked behind me once or twice, never really got used to it. Anyway, there was some hot cawl waiting for me at home, so I'd soon be fit to start another week.

I often think of Doll, and the big part she played in our education. The rides I had with her were far more interesting and pleasant than any rides the pupils have today in their school bus, I'm sure of it. Incidentally, Doll provided the same service for my eldest brother, when he went to Swansea to school to the old Higher Grade School, now Dynevor. He used to ride her to Killay on Monday mornings, though he used saddle and bridle. And with the same homing instinct she would get back to Ty'r-coed in three hours. In fact we heard later that sometimes she helped the postman to cover his rounds on Pengwern Common!

*

"Ibe gwain t'the Dog for a dobbin. If I beent back, thee zupper up the things. Tak'n and gie'n hafe a mawn and swedes apiece and dree ipsuns o'meal. Zthee knaw weh th' meal is? Pan top o' the tallat setps, in the keeve."

*

George Waters, local preacher: "Dost thee know, boy, there's only a paper partition between dancing and Hell? One wrong step and thee'rt through it!"

LIZZIE MORGAN

Boarding House Keeper
Born in Overton 1894

When I was a girl in the village I used to be very shy, until the war brought me out—the 1914 war, that is. After the war had been going a little time, one of the big houses here—Lulsley——was opened as a hospital, and I was taken on to look after the nurses at their cottage. "Well now, Lizzie" the Matron said, "you'll have to keep these nurses under", she said, "because if you don't, they'll be sure to keep you under". So I used to chase them and watch them like a hawk, to see they put things back in the pantry and all that. I was the cook, you see. As luck would have it, I had been helping for a few years with a posh family who used to take a house nearby, and one of the daughters spent a lot of time learning me to cook. So now I had to cook for twenty wounded soldiers, the night nurse, Matron and myself. I had to start before half past six every morning, light the old Eagle stove, sweep out the two front rooms, sweep the Matron's sitting room, do her fire if she had one, then cook her breakfast, all by half past eight, then cook the men's breakfast by nine. It was something of a convalescent home, really, for soldiers who had been wounded at the Front, some with their arms or legs off, or wounded in the head, and I had to do all the cooking. Food was rationed, of course, and I had to make up meals for them out of anything that was handy. A lot of maize puddings, and concoct things with lentils and I don't know what all, and for breakfasts they'd always have a great big saucepan of porridge. Possy they used to call it. They were always asking what mysteries they were having next . . . they said I was a good cook, I suppose you had to keep on thinking up meals for that crowd.

Besides the cooking, it was my job to clean the outside lavatories, earth closets they were, and that was a rotten job I can tell you, keeping those clean. I was at it from morning to night, in fact I was working so hard I found my legs starting to swell, so after that they gave me two hours off every afternoon. I was at this job for three and a half years, until it closed down. In the end I had to take my Red Cross nursing certificate. Oh yes, I felt quite close to the war in a way, though we were so far away from it.

I had the time of my life with those men at the hospital, I can tell you. There was a Mr Cooper, he was living in a cottage alongside, he was a retired gentleman, I think. He had plenty of money anyway. And he was always entertaining the soldiers, he would give them their Christmas dinner, for instance, and he would take them on outings, we'd go on the old bus to Worms Head, and there we'd have a big picnic on the cliff-top. I had to go with them everywhere, I was their mascot, they said. We went on trips to Swansea, and I remember going sometimes to the Empire Theatre, but because I wasn't in uniform I wasn't allowed in until I dressed up in someone else's uniform and his hat and coat. Then I'd pass as one of the men. I had two or three romances then, too. I was engaged to one boy from London, but I found out he was a boozer, so I chucked him. We had some Russians there, and Australians—they were getting a lot more pay than our boys and it made them jealous. It was a good time in my life, but it was a very hard time, too, by gum.

Peace Day was a day I'll never forget. The men were all so excited, "We're free now", they said, "we're going to cel-ebrate". The Matron said to me, "Are you coming over to the Ship with us, Lizzie?" "No", I said, "I can't go. I've got a milk pudding in the oven and I don't know what on the stove. I'll follow you later". But by the time I went over, the men were tumbling all over the Burrows, they were so tight. Then they made their way to the school house, and got hold of a big drum that was kept there, and they marched through the village thumping this old drum. There was a service on at the church at the time, and here was a Scots fellow outside singing "Stop yer tickling, Jock" on top of his voice and the congregation trying to sing a hymn inside. Then a message come through from Mr Pritchard, the Penrice agent, he phoned to say he was bringing some champagne down to celebrate, but by the time he come we couldn't find half the men, they were all up to here, tipsy.

*   *   *

We didn't spend so much time and money on entertainment in those old days of course. What there was would be centred around the chapel. Good Friday would be a big day. We'd have a tea on the cliffs and the superintendent used to learn us some new hymns to sing in the afternoon service. It was the only time in the year we used to have new dresses. Tea in the chapel, then out onto the cliffs to play Twos and Threes and Kiss in the Ring. In the winter we'd have concerts, and we'd have to learn recitations for them, then at Christmas there'd be the Christmas Tree. All chapel and Sunday School—there used to be nine different classes in those days.

I was married when I was thirty-three. My husband was twenty years older than me. He used to tell me that if he'd met me earlier I wouldn't be doing what I was doing. He was very good to me. Before ever I knew him he was a postman, from Porteynon, riding around Gower on a pony, for 5/- a week. He come down here after his wife died, and we were married, like that. He did know our family. My mother told me that when I was a little girl he took a fancy to me and wanted to adopt me! In 1928 he bought this big house I'm living in now, and we started taking visitors right away. The house is right on the beach, and we never had any trouble in filling it.

There've been holidaymakers in Horton for ages and ages and ages, and a few of the big houses would be let out to families for a month at a time. But what I did, was to do the cooking, while the visitors found the food. I kept it like that all the time, till recently. Hard work? People don't realise what it's like today. I did all the washing, cleaning, ironing, preparing different meals for different families. I was often out in the shed at eleven on a Saturday night feathering fowls for the Sunday dinner. I used to take about sixteen people here at a time. And I always used to give them big white tablecloths, white table napkins, and towels, I'd provide all them things. Yes, every meal, white things. I had seen that done, you see, in other houses, so I followed suit. I used to charge about £3 a week for a family, and that could be six or seven of them. Very little money we made. But we had some good class families coming here, some of them kept coming for twenty years, and more, every year, like

Horton Sunday School outing to Mumbles, 1906.

(Elizabeth (Lizzie Morgan (neé Roberts), back row 4th from left, and George Tucker, back row, extreme right).

clockwork. It was very interesting, mind, there'd be professors, and medical men, and preachers. I remember once Sir John Wolfenden stayed here, and when he was down on the beach one day he heard a girl screaming from the sea, she was drifting out on an airbed. He called out to her not to panic, he slipped his coat and hat off, and went in and saved her, brought her safely to shore. Anyway, she got onto the sand, then she walked off and never even said thank you to him.

The visitors didn't seem to mind that the house had no mod.cons. as they say. Just jugs and basins in the bedrooms. For years I used to carry the water up to them myself in the mornings. Rain water we used to collect in a cistern, otherwise my husband had to fetch it from the pump at the end of the lane. When the piped water came we had a tap fitted inside the garden gate, then later on the tap was brought into the kitchen. What was difficult to do for the same reason was keeping the outside closet clean. Every morning after I'd lit my fire I'd have to go down the garden with a bucket of water and some lime and that, empty it into a trench we had opened up and wash it out. Then

Old well, Horton.

dinner-time I'd pop down again, and again in the evening. To tell you the truth, I was often complimented on keeping my lavatory clean.

At any rate, eventually I had to pay out a lot of money and get a water closet built outside, and that's it there now. Cost me £89 that did.

Lamps again, they took a lot of time, keeping them clean and trimmed and filled, so after my husband went from us, I had the electric put in a few of the rooms. I've got one lamp left now, and I'm told it'd be worth about fifteen guineas.

*   *   *

The sea is at my doorstep, and I love that. When my husband was alive we used to go 'wrecking' together as far as Oxwich Point, two or three times a week. We'd carry back a load of useful sticks. That big wooden hut at the side of the house, we found most of that over in No Man's Land. We upended one piece after the other, all the way back. Then I used to pick laverweed from the rocks, regularly. To help out with the mortgage on the house I used to do a regular trade with the laverbread I made. I used to sell it to local people, four pence a pound. There'd be rather a lot of sand with the weed from round here, so I had to wash it first very thoroughly, three clean waters usually. Then I'd boil it in a saucepan for about two hours. Some would give it longer. I used to grease the saucepan well with a lump of lard, then add a good handful of salt. I always put a cloth over the saucepan while it is cooking, and as the weed reduces, the cloth sucks up the water that's come out. I keep rinsing the cloth out in cold water and squeezing it, then I put it back over the saucepan, and it helps to keep the laverbread dry. After that it would be minced up small, and that's that. Sometimes I'd collect carrageen from the rocks, too, this I'd wash and hang out to dry on paper until it is bleached to a cream colour. With a pint of milk that makes a good blancmange, great for invalids, that.

Oh, I love laverbread. Always have it in the house if I can. We

used to eat nettles, too, my husband and I. He used to think a lot
about herbs. Now he was a talented man, if you like. One thing
he was very gifted at was rhyming. He'd be talking to you now,
say, and the next minute he'd have a rhyme about you. When
the village hall was built, he made up a whole string of verses
about it and about the people of the village who were involved
in it, and at the opening he recited all this. Oh, he was at it for
years and years. At any rate, as I was saying, he was a great one
for herbs. One time he had water trouble, and he was supposed
to have an operation, but he used to take a sort of tea made from
cleavers—goose-grass they call it—and he found that very
good. Then a neighour got him a recipe and some herbs from
town, there was juniper berries and senna pods and that. I think
he took a few lots of that, and one day when he was down the
garden, something went click inside him, and he never had no
trouble with his water afterwards. Remarkable. Because there
was a time that, when he was in town, he couldn't pass a gents

but what he was in there. We used to collect and dry herbs then
—things for colds, like burdock, and agrimony, and yarrow,
and horehound. I had a little book with all these things in, and
recipes, but it got lost, and I'm sorry now. I could do with them
these days, with my knees and hands as they are. A tremendous
lot of people used to have faith in herbs and cures from nature,
you know. One woman I knew had cancer on her face, and she
was told that cow dung was a good remedy for it. At any rate,
she gave it a try, and indeed it worked. The cow dung cleared it
away completely. I think faith has got a lot to do with it, too.

GEORGE TUCKER

Builder
Born in Horton 1894

Life in this village was divided into two: by money. You had
the Bevans who had some and the Reeses who had none. Clear-
cut. When we went to chapel the rich ones sat in the front and
the poor ones in the back. I remember my father saying . . .
"We'll ha' to sit back here, boy, we can't go on with the
Bevans". What struck me very much as I got older was the
intermarriage. They couldn't go far enough away, you see. So
the poorer families were often below par, not all of them, but
there were quite a few village idiots, as they call them. On the
rich side there weren't so many, but there were some, and they
came mostly from cousins marrying cousins, to keep the
money in the family. I remember an old fellow saying to me:
"Well there you are, George", a said, "the Almighty don't
favour the rich or the poor when it comes to children. If they
intermarry, the children won't be up to much, I reckon. Now if
that were a farmer," a said, "he'd ha' sent off for a bull from
Hereford, or a ram from Brecon, but not these", a said, "so
these went under because they had plenty of money and wanted
to keep it in the family and these went under because they had
no money at all . . ."

The village was very small of course, and what I liked about it then was the people were all like one. My brother and me, say, we go up to the village to play—we were one of the few families who lived at the bottom, near the sea—and come dinner-time now, we wouldn't think of going home, you'd just go in the first house, and you'd have what they had. It might be only a culfer of bread and a bit of cheese and butter, but that's how it was. And if you were ill, see, the whole village seemed to feel it, like. Mind you, there'd be plenty of quarrelling, too, but if anything was the matter, or if anybody come in from outside, they'd close the ranks pretty sharp. Times were very hard then, but there'd always be help. John Bevan had a boat, down here at the quay, he used to catch fish for a living. It come on rough, and the boat got damaged, broken up, no good. He didn't have no money, of course, to buy a new boat. So what happened at a time like that, if a farmer lost a cow, or a horse the villagers would have a get-together, a bit of a concert, you see, and they'd

Sea Beach, Horton, early 1900s: George Tucker's grandmother (standing, extreme right) and mother (back row, extreme right).

make up enough of money to buy one in place, like. But this John Bevan had a bit of luck. I remember his wife telling me: "The other night I had a bit of luck, boy, I was coming from the quay past Well Stone, and there was a cask, washed up. I thought 'twas full of brandy or something, but I kicked 'n, and there wasn't no sound, so I tried to lift the blooming thing, but no, so we come back with a lantern and we rolled it up over the bank and we dug a hole, buried 'n till next morning. We went down now next day and opened 'n up—and twas full of bees-wax. Funny thing, wasn't it? So we got a bucket and carried it up a bit at a time, and I melted it down into half pound pats, in basins and that, and I tramped all over the place selling this beeswax"—4 shillings a pound I think she said—"and with that and what the villagers made we had enough to buy a boat".

Oh, yes, every village had its characters, and that made the places different, because it was the characters who were the dominant ones and everybody knew them. You've most likely heard of Sam Bevan, in Rhossili. Everyone would go to him for him to read the paper for 'em at the weekend. He was the best educated man in the parish, no doubt. I used to hear 'em say . . . "If you want to know anything, go out to Sam Bevan." Then there was Will o'Harepits, he was a local preacher, I remember him well. And he'd be up in the pulpit, with his hands holding the lamps, and he'd be almost crying, and saying how pleased he'd be when the time come to meet his Maker. Well, Will went to Swansea to live and one of the villagers told me: "Old Will o'Harepits, he'th a been very ill, thee's know, for a long time. I'th a heard 'n in the pulpit saying he'd be glad when the Lord'd come and tak'n . . . well, a said, a went to Swansea, and now he's spendin' all his blinking money, a said, on getting the doctors to keep 'n alive".

We used to laugh at all these old people, but in a way every one of them was more of an original thinker than what you get today. And some of them were terrors for practical jokes. Old Will o'Vernal (Fernhill), he used to go down to his neighbour's and sit on the settle outside the cupboard bed, he would sit there sometimes until dinner-time, to stop the old man getting up.

And there was Ellen and her three black pigs. The estate would rent you a pigshouse for a shilling a year, and Ellen she'd say to me: "Boy, I can't stop 'em eating, and what is three-pennorth o' meal", she said, "between three great colliers?" My wife came up with me one day, to buy a loaf of bread, from Ellen, and in the kitchen, hanging there, was one of these big pigs, twenty score or more, camered all out, and spread over in front, and Ellen said to my wife, who didn't know a thing about pigs, "Maid", she said, "now there's a fine pig for thee, tak off thee gloves now and feel the thickness of 'n . . ." But my wife wouldn't so much as touch 'n.

My grandfather now he was a wag too. A ship come ashore in Fall Bay, full of mutton it was . . . And the men come down there in the night and carried this mutton up, see, took it home, when who should appear on the skyline but a couple of preventive men, as they were called. My grandfather saw them as they were silhouetted against the moonlight, see, so he shouted out: "Don't come down, stop where you are! If you come a step further, you'll fall over these rocks and things, and break your necks . . . I'll come right up and show you the way down". "Right, thank you very much", was the reply. So my grandfather and his brother and the rest were able to unload themselves of the mutton and shove it into the furze, then they went up round and said . . . "Now, come down this way, sir, we'll take you down where 'tis safe" . . . and as far away from the mutton as possible . . .

Another day grandfather came out of Corner House just as the old German Maier come along with his wife. He used to sell fish, and mend clocks and buy rabbit skins and things like that. His wife used to drive the cart and sell the fish . . . she only had one arm. Just as he come out, a brake-load of men was going home, from The Ship, well away, swinging along, when the driver of the brake swerved and the hub of his wheel hit Ellen Maier's cart and broke the shaft. Ellen went sprawling, and just as the driver was about to make off, my grandfather stopped him: "Don't you go from here . . . just look what you've done!" And he pulled up the empty sleeve of Ellen Maier's coat . . . "You've gone and cut her bloody arm off, that'a what you've

Four generations of Tuckers. From right to left: George Tucker, his son Ivor, his father, and his grandfather.

done . . .''. This frightened the driver, of course, and he thought, ''I'll have to do something about this''. ''All right'', said my grandfather, ''you make a whip round for poor old Ellen, and we won't say a word about it.'' So they sent the hat round and gathered a tidy few bob, and ''Now, off you go'', a said, ''and mum's the word''.

There were really nippy characters about then, in every village. Of course, they lived in times when you had to be quick and agile in mind to get by. Honest, and cheerful mind, but deep as the sea, you'd have a job to get to the other side of 'em. But no doubt about their honesty, they'd rather give than take any day. Say you wanted a pair of boots from Swansea. You'd say to the busman . . . ''Go to Bosby's, boy, and get me a pair of dowled boots size nine and tell 'n I'll pay when I come in''. Bosby's would send the boots down, though I might not be going in for six months. D'you see. Or ''go to Griffiths the Ironmonger and ask 'n to send us down twelve pound of brown paint, pay you when I come in''. They'd send it, no question at all. Sometimes the busman would pay himself for you. Everyone was depend-

ent on everyone else, like. There was a sense of collectiveness.
In one village, that is, but not between the villages. Between
Porteynon and Horton, now, there's always been an underlying
rivalry. They'd never cooperate in anything. No good having a
combined social, nobody'd go. Even at Coronation time the
two villages wouldn't come together, and it's pretty well the
same today. And as far as the villages in North Gower are concerned, they were absolute foreigners to us.

When I went to the school at Porteynon it was run by the
Estate, and the Church. The Estate used to buy all our slates
and books and pencils, and they picked the teachers. And you'd
only get the job if you went to church, mind. Qualifications
were secondary. We had quite a good old schoolmaster, he
could take us up to multiplication and division of money, we
didn't go further than that, you see, because the old man
couldn't do it himself. And every morning Parson Price would
come up and give us a lesson on the Scriptures, then we'd have
an examination on that every year, for a Bishop's Certificate.
But the funny thing about it, see, the chapel children were
better at it than the Church children, I think because the Nonconformists were pretty strict with you. I'd have to read the
Bible, lor, whether I wanted to or not. Chapel three times a Sunday and you'd be talking about these things, but the Church
children, they'd only read the Bible in Sunday School, like, so
the old parson, he'd come and say . . . "Oh, now, that's a very
good girl. She's not up to much in examinations, but she comes
to church, and she really ought to have a certificate", and the
examiner'd say . . . "Well I think we'd better give her one". And
even if she didn't know Moses from the Revelations she'd get a
certificate, you see. As I say our schoolmaster was quite good,
but he was very cruel, he used to beat us unmercifully. I
remember telling his daughter long after his time: "Well if
there's a Hell, your old man is there right enough". He
wouldn't even let us have our sandwiches and that in the school
. . . "twill gather the mice". So we'd be sent outside in all
weathers, to manage somehow in the cold and wet under the
hedge.

I left school at fourteen and I went into farm service in Overton. I worked twelve months for £8. Very hard work. Some days I'd start from here with a couple of cattle or sheep and off we'd go, to the butchers, at Killay. We'd walk them all the way, then we'd have to walk all the way back. The roads were rough and our boots were dowel boots, kip leather and that, and by the time we got home we'd be dropping. I remember the first day that Johnny Grove bought a new bus, I was given a shilling to pay for a ride home, but he never turned up, and I was left in Killay. So I walked home, of course, twelve miles. When I came to the Towers I was half afraid to go down past the castle, the old mill was so creepy, and the White Lady would be waiting at the stile near Hangman's Cross . . . I tiptoed all the way past it all, and got home about midnight, I was so blinking tired. I had a cup of tea, and the farmer said to me: ''Well, George, I haven't suppered-up yet, get the lantern, and we'll go and supper-up the things'' . . . after the day I'd had! Another time I went with the farmer to a place outside Llanelli. I took the horse and trap to Loughor, left it in a stable, and walked out after some sheep. We put the lambs up in the trap then, the ewes would walk behind. The farmer got in, but he made me walk all the way back . . . never offered me a lift . . . every step of the way I followed the trap . . . can you imagine that happening today?

The only work for men in those days was farming, that and a bit of quarrying. Dick Robert, for instance, he used to get up at four in the morning when he was a young man and he would mow an acre of hay for 2/6, that was by hand with a scythe, and it would take him most of the day. If you were mowing corn, you'd put a 'cradle' on the scythe, and that would leave enough of corn to bind it by hand, and for that you'd get six-pence extra. You'd be expected to turn your hand to anything, reap and mow, thatch, thresh, by hand, with a threshel as we called it.

The Gloy-mow

Gloy was different to the ordinary straw. When they'd be threshing barley and oats the men who was cutting the sheaves on the top of the machine would throw them in any shape, heads down first, so it would beat out the heads better. But when you're threshing wheat, you'd want the wheat straw, for thatching the ricks or the roofs of cottages, so then it'd be put in length-ways into the drum and it'd go down through, the heads would thresh off in the usual way, and the straw would carry out over the bosses at the back of the machine, where the men would be catching it, and then they'd catch it straight as it come out and bind it into big sheaves. That was called gloy. And they'd make these gloy-mows in the rickyard different shape to the rest of them. The big sheaves would be put crosswise, so that when it came to 'drawing gloy' as they called it, the big sheaves would be separated into small ones and they'd be raked out; they'd have rakes with long teeth and they'd rake out all the weed and all the filth and they'd straighten out the gloy into small sheaves, and this'd be called 'reed', and for putting on the ricks they wouldn't be very big. It'd be just enough when they were open to complete the thatching of the rick and if it was for thatching a cottage they'd make it very straight, but generally in my time, I've been at it, they'd thresh it on a cask in the barn, spread canvas on the floor, knock out all the heads and keep the straw as straight as they could. The grain and the husk would be put into a wimmelling machine and that would separate it out just as the threshing would. That was called 'drawing gloy'. They would pull out the big sheaves as they went along. This was a 'gloy-mow' and not a straw-rick.

For hoeing swedes you'd get a penny for forty yards. My, the farmer was too hard a master for me. I was pulling swedes for the sheep one day, and the ground was frozen so hard, I couldn't get any out, and he came up. I was only 15 then and I was starving cold, but he was holding forth and that, and I had a quick temper, and, anyway, I suddenly had enough, I threw stones at him and went off, left him. That was when my career in farming came to an end and I began to learn my trade as a carpenter.

Up to the 1950s of course your farm was almost certain to belong to the Penrice Estate. And, as far as estates go, it wasn't bad. They looked after their tenants. But you had to toe the line, mind. If you crossed their path, shot a pheasant, say, you'd lose your farm. Like that. But they employed quite a few of the villagers, I think there were twenty-two working in the castle, and the woods, in the churchyards, and the farms, doing repairs, but not many of those. The main thing was that every farmer had to go cap in hand for anything he wanted. He couldn't do as he liked, he couldn't sell what he liked. Evan Morgan of Pitt, he thought he'd go in for a bit of market gardening, on his own, and he sold a few parsnips and carrots and swedes. He got notice to quit. He'd broken the conditions. So he had to leave, he went to London and he bought seven acres of land out in Hertfordshire or somewhere and he went in for growing flowers. Miss Talbot did write to him to say she was sorry, but it was too late then.

They charged very little rent but didn't do much to the cottages in the way of repair, so they got dilapidated, and if you wanted a new grate or a new oven put in, there'd be a year's rent gone. And 'twas easy to quarrel with the agent. I was a socialist and that was a terrible thing in those days. And I was a local preacher with the Methodists. If you were doing something for the church, now, you'd get plenty of help, like the hall in Porteynon. But chapel people got precious little help from them. Oh, we did have a do at Penrice once a year, Miss Talbot would invite all the school children to the castle. And we'd have tea and some bread and jam and a great big bun with a currant here and there. I said to one chap, if you gave one of these to your Rhode Island Reds, they wouldn't touch 'n, but we're supposed to be glad to get 'n. That was the feeling, see. A sort of undercurrent. I think people grew up to get used to it. It was that or quarrying, or catching rabbits. If you had a farm you even had to have written permission to catch a blooming rabbit! And as for the pheasants . . . they had three or four keepers and they'd go round and gather up all the cluppit hens, give you a couple of bob for one, then they'd put a hen to sit on the pheasants' eggs. You could have her back then, after, for a shilling, but by that time she wouldn't be much good. She wouldn't lay for a couple of months and there was nothing on her to eat.

When Miss Talbot was at Penrice, usually for the 'shoot', she'd drive round in her carriage to inspect the estate. Old Pritchard on his white horse, he'd go along in front, you see,

and say you were on the road, pulling dung perhaps, he'd stop
you and say: ''Pull into the field there, boy, make way for her
ladyship'' . . . and you had to get off the road and let Miss Talbot
drive by. I'm afraid that sort of thing got me. It was a sort of
cloud over you. But, mind you, 'tis a funny thing, when she
sold off the estate and the tenants came to own their farms, the
outlook altered overnight. Nothing changed the Gower people
more than this: suddenly they had their freedom to be little
landlords theirselves, a lot of them, anyway. Now they could
spend their money, and change things on the farm and argue the
point. Before that you never heard a squeak out of them. But
now . . . they were going to do this, and that . . . they were cocks
on their own dunghill now . . . ''Now you can't come this way.
This bit of field belongs to me'' . . . in fact, they were worse, you
see, they were so petty, like. They were all cock-a-hoop now
and a darn sight worse than the Estate had ever been! Not that
the farming improved all that much. Until recently it's been
very lacksadaisical in Gower. No business in it at all. Today the
farmer wouldn't have a minute to give you, then the next two
days he'd be standing around doing nothing. A Gower farmer
always had time to stand and talk.

Nothing played a greater part in the economics of a Gower-
man than his pig. Everybody had to have a pig. There was more
discussion about pigs after chapel on Sunday morning than
there was about the sermon. Reports, comparisons, my grandfather used to tell me: ''If anybody asks you to guess the weight
of his pig'', he said, ''always judge 'n high, you'll be their friend
for life''. It was a way of life, you see. You'd buy a pig for ten
shilling, eight week old, and you'd keep 'n then for the best part
of twelve months, or more, and by that time he'd get to twenty
to twenty-two score in weight, a heavy pig, that. Then the time
come to kill your pig. You'd get him out of the pigshouse,
which would be quite small, by putting a slip knot over his
mouth, tie him round the jaw so he couldn't bite, because
they're very strong animals, and would bite, too. Then two or
three fellows would get him out and alongside of a bench, a
special bench for the job, with short legs, only about a foot high,
because you had to roll 'n up, you see, onto this bench, on his

side. Some butchers used to kill em standing up, but with a big pig that was a nasty job. You've got your pig now on his side, with three or four fellows now lying on him, and the butcher would stick him, under the throat. Right, so far so good. One of the women would be there, catching the blood . . . while it was running it had to be mixed fast. Most women would mix it with their hands, to keep it fluid, whisk it round to stop it kietching, because once it kietched, 'twas no good. Then that blood would be used for making blackpot.

The next thing was scraping the pig. We used to do that with the old-fashioned tin candlestick, the sort that had a middle part where you could rise the candle up or down. The bottom would be like the cover of a tin, about four inches across. In Pembrokeshire they usually used the covers of tins. You couldn't use a butcher's knife, because it would cut the skin. So the candlestick was kept for the job. And it was essential to use scalding water, and that's not boiling water, mind. Scalding is a degree or so under. The butcher would make sure the water was boiling in the copper, then he'd take out a canful and try one leg of the pig in it, adding a drop of cold water to it. As soon as ever he'd find the hairs coming off easy, he'd start on the job, one leg at a time. There'd be a few fellows scraping the bristles off and the loose skin. It's amazing what could be done with what came from a pig . . . First thing, there's always a couple of bristles at the back of the neck, longer than any others, about two, two and a half inches long. They'd be carefully saved for the cobbler. To make what he called his wax end. He'd cut off three or four lengths of his point thread, that's a very strong roughish thread, then he'd take the wax he'd made, out of tar and one or two other ingredients, and when it was pliable he'd pull it along these point threads and roll them on his knee till he'd have what he called a wax end, very strong. That's what he used to sew on the soles of boots or put a patch on a toe-cap on. When you made a hole with an awl, then, you couldn't get it through, so he'd take one of the pig's bristles and work it and roll it in. Then he could get the thread through the hole.

What else? Well, you'd hang her up now, on a cameral, that was a wide piece of timber with squotches, or catches, on it.

The legs of the pig would be hung up on this, out like that, and the Achilles heel would be cut. Then you'd clean the pig inside, cut him down very carefully in the front and bring all the innards out into a big bath. Nothing was wasted. Some of the gut, about one inch across, would be saved for the blackpot. And the smaller gut, there'd be two or three yards of it, that would be the right size for sausage. They'd turn the gut inside out and clean it with an old blunt knife, scald them first. For blackpot now, the blood would be boiled, and into it would go your sage and your thyme and your oatmeal to thicken it. Boil it all up then fill a length of the gut with the mixture, tie it up and hang it on a rod over the fireplace to dry. Then you could cut off a piece if you wanted to fry some with your bacon. That was the blackpot.

What we used to call the mow-pot was made from the main gut. This would be cut up into small pieces and fried with your bacon. Chittlings was another name for that. Then they'd save the ears, they'd save the trotters, and the tail. They'd make two cuts, one each side of the backbone and you'd have a long wedge the length of the pig, and that's called the chine. When the pig was salted, the chine would be left till last, on the top. You'd have the steak, you'd have the spare ribs, very nice they were too, and the butcher would put aside a few odds and ends for you to cook for the Sunday. Then the chine would be lightly salted, and that would last you a couple of weeks, you'd roast this, but 'twasn't the best roasting piece, I reckon. You'd put the bacon down, the hams on top of the bacon, with salt and a bit of salt-petre around the knuckle, that's where 'twould go first. Then after three weeks, you'd wash it off and hang it up in the charnel to dry, one ham each side of the fire and the flitches up in the charnel. And that would last a small cottager . . . twenty score, you see . . . well, till a pig come again.

Mind you, it'd be very salt . . . I couldn't eat it myself, but it was the thing, you see, cabbage, and bacon and potatoes, once or twice every week, apart from a bit of fried bacon and egg. And the way of doing the bacon was, instead of putting it on top of the fire like with the old griddles, you'd do it in front of the fire. Break the egg on a plate and toast the bacon so that the fat would drop onto the egg and cook it, see. The two'd be ready then the same time.

Then there was any amount of rabbits. They were more or less a staple diet. I had so many on the first farm I worked at, I never wanted to see one since. I'd even touch my hat on 'n if I saw one getting away. We used to have rabbit every day. Even if we had meat we'd have a rabbit cooked in with it. They were a real menace in these parts, I've seen fields of corn practically ruined by rabbits. They'd be breeding, you see, just when the corn'd be growing best. You have a field of eight to ten acres and for four or five yards from the hedge, very near a quarter of the field, you'd get nothing. And 'twasn't only what they'd eat. The blooming things, nothing would eat after them, see, they'd more or less poison the grass. I wasn't keen on the old myxomatosis, mind, but 'twas a real good thing to get rid of 'em. But boy, you'd never get on top of 'em, you could look into this field and it'd be alive with rabbits, right down to the sea. There's a few coming back now, but funny thing, they're not so wild as they used to be, almost as if they didn't know what a human being was. And they don't go into the ground so much, they're more in the bushes, like a hare now. No big buries (burrows) in the hedge like there used to be. I don't think there was any sentiment lost on rabbits round here. The countryman that's

brought up with the animals, I think he may feel a bit of kind-ness towards ponies and horses, but on the whole, he's different from the townsman. He'd have no sympathy with a cow or a sheep or a pig, because that was to kill for meat and that was all about it. He wouldn't lose no sleep over them going to the slaughter-house. Indeed, 'tis almost the same with dogs especially sheep dogs. Once he come that he can't follow the sheep and do his job, they'd say, ''best thing thee canst do is tak'n away and shoot 'n, he's of no account any more''. Tisn't cruelty, really. The dog is part of the farm and its life. A bit hard-hearted maybe. Or we're getting softer. Take birds, for instance, in the country. We feed the birds on our lawn here, that comes in. Now when I was a boy, if there was a bird in our garden, the first thing my father'd do was try to kill 'n, throw a stone or something. A blackbird was nothing but enemy number one, he'd be after the gooseberries or the blackcurrants, see. And if the cat caught a few birds, that was a good cat. And if the cat couldn't catch 'em, they'd kill the cat.

Like most of the village boys then I had no ambition other than to go to farm service. I really did want to be a farmer, I liked farming, I liked animals. But as I told you I left farming for good when I was 15 and I went to learn a trade. Here again a country boy would be at a disadvantage. The amount a country carpen-ter could teach you was limited. You'd learn how to make field gates, ladders, how to repair carts, how to make mangers and stillings and partitions, that would be most of the work, and you'd go round repairing for the Estate, stable and cowshed doors and that sort of thing. But I was lucky in a way, I come on the scene just at a time of change in building, and there was a few houses being built. So I had the chance of learning how to make doors and windows, all by hand, out of deal, and although the carpen-ters round about were very ordinary there were some jobs like that to be done by hand they could do very well. Then the gen-eral run was to go into Swansea and start as an 'improver'. So I went into a small business and there I got the rough edges knocked off, like. No machinery, of course, but you'd get a lot more windows to make and that, and I learned how to make stairs, different shapes and sizes and different rises and so on.

So when I come back to the village, after the War that was, I built most of the new houses round here. Better I'd never seen some of them, because I couldn't sell 'em after I'd built 'em. Bad time it was. And to think of it, one I built up the hill there for £500 was sold recently for £24,000! I will say this, mind. I think, when a country carpenter really learned his trade, he'd often be better than a town boy. Keener on his job for one thing doing what he wanted to do. But the snag with me was, I felt I was very backward, I'd only had my education in the Church School here, as I told. So, I went to night school for two winters, Geometry and Building Construction. The teacher went out of his way to help me, because when it come to putting it down on paper, I was lost. Bottom of the class. But because I really wanted to do it, when it come to the tests I wasn't right at the bottom. So I bought some books and studied them, did bits on my own, and when I went back the second winter I wasn't so lost, and soon I come to draw up my own plans and set out my own jobs. I really did work hard mind. But I'd never been trained, see, to count quick or see things quick.

The only other work I could have done in the village was quarrying, but that wouldn't have got me very far. Even if I could have got it. It always struck me as being comical that if you were a good worker, the Estate would let you have a quarry, and if you know of anything harder than quarrying stones by hand . . .! With the old jumper, boring the holes down, and yet, see, there was no shortage of men to do it, women, too, they used to load up the boats. My grandmother used to go down to the quars at Rhossili, with a number of the young women, and load boats, with anything up to 90 to 100 tons of stone, load them by night, and they'd get 9d. The men used to go out onto Worms Head, they'd catch some rabbits, or hares or pheasants, then they'd walk into Swansea with them, sell them, walk back and bring home the powder they'd have bought, back to the Ship Inn at Middleton. The limestone trade, of course, is the chief reason why 80% of Gower people came from the other side of the water. We're most of us mongrels, no doubt, but they do say the mongrel does better than the pure bred, I don't know . . .

I'm not sure what talents I had, really. Gift of the gab p'rhaps. I got to have a strong feeling for the community and . . . I'll say this about myself, I do like helping people if I can. For forty-five years I was a district councillor, so I had plenty of opportunity for that. Only fought one election. I was interested in education, for over twenty years I was chairman of the Education Committee. But when they put me as a representative on the Council of the University at Swansea, I found I hardly knew what they were talking about, I was out of my depth. So I chucked my hand in. I never believed in sitting listening to things that I can't properly grasp.

At the end of the War, too, I was made a magistrate. Me, rebel that I was! But I was very proud of that, I was the first working man to become a magistrate on the local bench. At first I had no idea of the thing, and I found it hard. Nowadays they give you a little handbook, but there was nothing then. Still, once I got to grips with things, I got to enjoy it—as far as one can enjoy that sort of job—but I did feel I was fulfilling a need. You see, I could put myself in the place of half of them people that was coming up in front of me. 'Twas easy for me to put myself in the place of a poacher, because I'th a been a poacher all my life. We had a man up before us, for poaching. There was Jack Bevan and me, I was chairman by now, and Jack was the vice-chairman. The fellow didn't live far from here. And the keeper was there, and the policeman. They'd caught this poor chap coming away with a couple of rabbits and I said to Jack under my breath: "Look, Jack," I said, "we'll have to stop this. We can't have this chap pinching our rabbits, 'twill never do, boy". And Jack said to me: "Ay, we'll have to stop 'n, George boy, because you see he's on our ground".

We had a fellow feeling, you see, and that is the whole idea of what you might call amateur magistrates . . . You'd get one J.P., he'd say: "Oh yes, no doubt about it, this man is guilty . . . don't like the look of him, bit of a blackguard, we'll fine him ten pounds". Now it didn't strike me like that, you see, I'd say: "Look, it's harder for that man to find thirty bob than 'tis for you to find ten pounds. Ask him what he gets per week, and give him a fortnight's fine". Relate a fine to what he could pay, that's all you can do, I reckon. I was pretty fiery myself once, I know how easy it is to say the wrong thing, do the wrong thing, so I always tried to put myself in the place of the man in front of me. I had two judges on the bench with me and I would always offer them the chair, but they'd never take it, they'd sit alongside me and help. Them fellows were wonderful men. I always tried to be unbiassed—Jack Bevan reckoned I was too unbiassed—but I had this fellow feeling I told you about.

I believe it was tied up, too, with being a local preacher, with the Methodists, for over fifty years. When I started, religion was very strong, or at least chapel-going was—though I sometimes think now that a good many became Methodists not so much out of the Love of God as out of fear of hell-fire. Heaven and Hell were very real places. The sermons of some of the local preachers in those days, my word, you would be very near hot and burning from the talk about Hell by the time you were out of chapel. I had no real intention of becoming a local preacher, but during the First World War I was working for the Admiralty at Pembroke Dock, and I joined a Mission that met in a loft and took a service or two, myself. So when I come back to Gower in the early 1920s, and the minister asked me if I'd go ''on trial'', I decided to have a go. I went round with another local preacher, I read the lesson a bit or said a prayer and said a few words, then I had a sort of examination at a special meeting, none of us had much idea of the theology of the thing, mind, but I don't think they cared, as long as they thought you'd be good enough, and be keen. Then you'd be put on the plan, like . . . Sundays were pretty tough going, no transport like today.

My father used to walk to Llangennith in the morning, seven or eight miles, often again in the evening. But whatever you say about these old fellows, they were very serious chaps, very sincere. Same with the villagers, if there was a special effort, say, Missionary Fund or something, they would always stretch a point, see. They were poor, they didn't have much to give away, but they would help and help and help. People will give today, but it seems to me they don't make a sacrifice. They don't help till it hurts, like those people did.

My father said to me once, about preaching: ''You see, boy, no two sermons are the same. Ten thousand thousand are our texts, but all our sermons one'', and there was a lot in that. One of the things I would try to do, and that was not to get stereotyped, not to repeat myself. Because you'd hear the locals say: ''Look out, Tom C. is here tonight, a preaches too long and we all know what a's going to say''. A lot of the old people didn't mind, though, they weren't exactly sermon-tasters, you could say what you liked and they'd be happy.

Something that's pleased me though is that some people have remembered what I've said in the pulpit, however trivial. One time I preached on a strange text from Jeremiah: ''The bed was too short for a man to lie on and the sheet too short to cover him''. I had come down the Swansea Valley, you see, and on a hoarding there was an advert for soap, someone had used the wrong soap and it had shrunk the quilt or something, and the comment struck me: ''When the sheet is short the bed seems too long'' . . . and that was before I'd seen the text from the Bible. Anyway the pith of my sermon was that people try to keep theirselves warm in this world with sheets that was too short, so they didn't rest properly, or take their religion seriously. And years after that I'd get comments from people I met: ''Now, George, see that thee sheet is long enough'' or ''see that thee bed don't get too short''—and I'd know what they were getting at.

Another time I was preaching about Jacob. Now our forefathers wouldn't have anything said against Jacob. But that wouldn't do me. I'd start by saying: ''Jacob'', I said, ''was the biggest twister in the Old and the New Testaments, there's very few of you here today who's a bigger twister than Jacob.'' I went on to show how Jacob twisted his father, his brother, his Uncle Laban and right up to the very end he even wrestled with God and wouldn't let him go unless he blessed him—so he really was a twister all his life. ''But what you've got to remember,'' I said, ''is that because God loved Jacob the twister, then there's a chance for us.'' And do you know, for years after that, right up until they died, if I met some villagers on the road, they's often call out: ''How's old Jacob getting on?'' ''Hello, boy, is Jacob any better?'' I didn't mind that, you see, because I knew they'd been listening. You like to feel that somewhere along the line you might have done some good, that something have rubbed off onto someone else.

I was preaching in Swansea one Sunday night, and there was a man in the gallery, I never knew his name. I could tell he didn't belong to the chapel . . . anyway, he didn't take his eyes off me, and outside the chapel after I could see he had dished himself up a bit to come to chapel at all, he looked as if he had a borrowed collar on, his coat was frayed and his boots were broken, but he come on to me "I'm glad I came tonight," a said, "I haven't been to chapel for very many years", a said, "now I've lost my job, I've lost my wife, I've lost my family. And I'd made up my mind to do away with myself", a said, "I was going round the town trying to earn a couple of shillings, sticking notices through people's doors, and I met one man who told me to come along here . . . 'there's a fellow from Gower there on Sunday,' he said, 'if you listen to him he's bound to do you a bit of good'". So he came. And I remember my text, I preached on Hope. You know the famous picture? There's a fellow playing a violin, but all the strings are broken, bar one, and he's doing his best on his one string. Hope, you see. So I said to 'n: "There you are, boy, you may have got only one string left on your fiddle, but there's always Hope, so keep trying!" And this man, he was overwhelmed by this, it seems. He told the man who'd sent him, who told me, that it had meant a new life for him. A simple little thing, but when you look back, you like to think that you may have helped somebody.

As I said, in my preaching I tried to be different. All them old stories, the lost sheep, the lost sixpence, the Prodigal Son, they've all been done to death, and always treated in the same way, sentimentalised, like. It's what happens in the world today that counts. So I'd take, say, the Prodigal Son story, and preach a sermon on the Elder Brother, he was a snake if you like. And there's more Elder Brothers about than Prodigal Sons, hardly a family without one. He's never got enough. Then take Jonah in the belly of the whale, nobody believes that any longer, but you see, if we do wrong, we are like Jonah, there's no way out, you see. Till we come to ourselves, and own up, then we see the light and we're saved. The way I've heard that preached about, in the end I don't know whether I'm more sorry for the whale than for the fellow inside. And to tell the truth, with more education today and common sense, we don't believe these stories any more, like we used to.

But I always had a liking for the odd way of looking at things —like my grandfather. He was full of unusual theories. But with my father, he was a local preacher, he had a one-track way of looking at things, so that I was brought up pretty narrow. And I used to find myself fighting against it. So later on, when I was making a sermon, I tried to be original, like, and I think it was effective, people had got tired of the same approach to the gospels. In Christianity, you see, it's only the Spirit that matters, the Holy Ghost. Look at it any other way and it's nothing but fairy stories. But something that strikes to the root of you, now, like great music, the Messiah, say, or a great work of art, then you get something that you can adapt to your own life. Touches you on the inside, like.

Of course, being right on the coast has had a tremendous influence on the history of this village, more than any in Gower, I reckon. The sea was where everyone wanted to go, to work. Not only the oyster boats, which was before my time, or the limestone boats, or the bricks and tiles from Bridgwater. We had a lot of 'blue-water' men as they were called, and at least half a dozen sea-going captains in the village, all deep sea. There was old Captain Stephens, he lost all his toes with frostbite down in the South Seas, I remember him telling me. Copper trade from Swansea a lot of them, all sailing ships. Sailing round the Horn. They'd be away for between twenty months and two years. Captain Bevan was always wanting me to go with him. Good job I didn't—only yesterday I was sea-sick in a boat not ten yards from the shore. A lot of these chaps became sea-men because their fathers were at sea. But they were special men, mind, you had to be pretty clever to be captain of a sailing ship. When Captain Bevan came home, everybody wanted to have a chat with him, and he'd bring home curios he'd picked up. It was a good job, mind, and pretty well paid.

I remember the boats bringing coal, and superphosphate and bricks from Bridgwater, a poor sort of brick they were, too fine, —they had twenty holes in them and the plaster wouldn't stick on 'em. And you'll see a lot of houses with the red tiles from Bridgwater, they were of softish clay and didn't last so well, got discoloured.

Some names of families about here too, they came from men who had come by the boats to work for the Castle, they'd come to clean out the fish-ponds and that, Brooke, Moore, Christian, Burton, Christmas, they're not Gower names at all. And the names of some houses. *Ciampa* was the name of Captain Bevan's boat.

On a coast like this, and navigation being what it was, you could always expect a wreck or two every winter. I remember one boat come ashore at Oxwich Point, loaded with fire bricks, and for a long time the men used to walk out there and carry one or two back. They were very good bricks; my father was a mason, and he'd line the ovens, for baking bread, with these bricks. And there was a lot of chimneys built with them. They were very heavy things, and three would be the most anyone could carry back, the three miles from the Point, but they used to do it, look. And up to recently you'd find a chance brick there from time to time, jammed in the rocks.

Another ship come ashore in the same place, she was loaded with copper ore. They piled up this copper, see, in one of the little bays, Lucas Bay, and ran a line of sorts to carry the ingots back into the big bay. One old fellow told me they tore your clothes to pieces, the edges were so sharp. The piece of ground they stacked them up on was about forty to fifty feet long and twelve to fifteen feet wide, and do you know, right up to today nothing have grown on that patch, only a bit of scrubby grass. You can see where it has poisoned everything. It killed the fern, it killed the weed, it killed the whole ground. And if you went up now you'd have no trouble in picking out that square. It must have gone down very deep. There's the patch. All fern, furze, grass, all gone. For many years there wasn't even any grass. Just the bare earth.

Then there was the *Duisberg*, she was loaded with deals.

Whether the captain didn't want to go to sea or not, I don't know, but the tugs came down to pull her off, the *Africa* and the *Challenger*, their names have stuck with me. Anyway, they towed the boat off, right. She wasn't holed, she wasn't nothing, but blow me, she came ashore again, on the sand in front of us here, in the bay. And they couldn't shift her from there, she'd settled in the sand. So they got rid of a lot of her deal, you could buy them very cheap, and in the end there was enough of blooming deals to build houses from here to Swansea.

The *Agnes Jack* was before my time, but we can't forget it because of the monument in the churchyard at Porteynon. My father told me about it: the sad thing was, the rocket was here, but they couldn't get at the boat. The sea was too wild, and the men got swept away when they were clinging to the masts, in full view of those on the shore. Charlie Bevan wrote a poem about it, with a bit of help I should think, I never knew him to be very much of a one for making up verse. And there are a few lines of the poem on the statue in the churchyard at Porteynon. On a slate slab you see the names of the crew, eighteen of them: "Oh had there been a lifeboat there, to fight the roaring main . . ."

It was because of the *Agnes Jack* that Trinity House put a lifeboat here. *The Daughter's Offering* came in 1884. But in 1916 that was lost, too, as is well-known.

When I was fourteen I used to drive the horses that pulled the boat to the water. There were six of them, and it was a big old job. With the first boat we used to go out into the sea with the horses until they'd be swimming, see. Then you'd turn 'em round and make the boat turn in the sea. And those on the beach would have to help to shove it as well. But with the second boat, the *Janet* it was different. We used to turn her on the sands, take the horses out of the shafts and hitch them alongside of the boat, there was two big loops on the back wheels. Then out they'd go. It was difficult because the blinking horses didn't like the noise, you see, these things used to clap as the wheels went round and the old horses would pull off at a tangent, like, a deuce of an old job.

The night the *Janet* was lost I got home from Swansea too late to go in her. Otherwise I'd have been a volunteer, no doubt, though I was no sailor. My mother was very glad, anyway. They were short of volunteers that night, because the older men didn't want to go. Even the sailors wouldn't have anything to do with it. And old Sam Gibb, that was Billy's brother, said that nobody ought to have went out, suicide to go, her said. But Billy was like that, you see, he was a nice old chap, but a bit foolhardy, like, nothing seemed impossible to him. So they had a couple of youngsters to fill up. Jack Morris, well, he didn't know one end of an oar from the other. And Will Grove, his father was in the boat.

The ship that come ashore was in the broken water along the coast here. Well, what happened, I suppose Billy ought to have known better. But he went into this broken water. She was a self-righting boat, so she'd have rode the swells well enough. But once in where the waves were breaking, nothing would stop her from going over. And so it was. They were lucky they wasn't all drowned. One or two of them held on and went around with the boat. Actually they should have all clung on to the thwarts and taken their chance, but no doubt they got thrown out, see, and jumped. There was three of them drowned, and strangely enough they were three of the most experienced boat men: Bill Gibb, coxswain; Will Eynon, the bowman, and George Harry, that had been out all his life. But the youngsters, look, who didn't know much about boating, they managed to survive. There you are. Well, that was the last we saw of a lifeboat. Because nobody wanted one any more. Even the experienced sailors wouldn't take on the responsibility.

Being near the sea have meant, too, you see, that since before 1900 we've had people coming here on their holidays. Not so many at first, of course. Going back now to when there was no motor-buses. And no 'guest-houses' as we know them now. You were a 'lodger' then and villagers would let the rooms or the house to you at about £1 a room. And do your cooking for you if you wanted. People would come from Bristol or Birmingham and that, and the busman would meet the train with his wagonette. Big job. They were generally fair-sized families that would take three to five bedrooms, and often they'd bring their servants with them. Stay for a fortnight or a month. Pretty well-

Billy Gibbs.

to-do usually. And these would come back year after year, because they'd have a good welcome, you see, and it was a great place for children, of course. Then after the First World War it seemed to change. One or two went into boarding . . . then they started 'guest-houses', that was a bit swankier, and ever since it's been like that, a common living room. Though a few haven't changed at all, even now. A lot more people come here now, but for shorter spells, and they don't anchor themselves here like they used to. Mind, you don't get the same kind of visitor. The old ones, after a couple of years, they'd get to know everybody—they'd have to go to the shop, or get the milk theirselves, consequently half the pleasure they'd get would be to become part of the village, and the children would go and buy a pennorth of sweets. It was part and parcel of their holiday. And the villagers used to look forward to their lodgers, good heavens above. They'd talk about the visitors as if they belonged to them. If they didn't come they'd say: "How been't they here this year? I wonder what's up with they?"

All different now, with the caravans. I've got an open mind on the caravans. I know that when we kept the shop here, there

Lifeboat practice at Porteynon, 1916.

Lifeboat practice at Porteynon with Billy Gibbs as Coxswain.

was no bigger boon to us than the caravanners. They'd be in the shop two or three times a week and they brought a tremendous lot of money to the place. I don't want to see the countryside destroyed. I've fought for this village for forty years. But you take Porteynon. The two shops there are not too well off, so the caravans in the summer are almost their livelihood. See what it means to them, or the pub, or the ice-cream man—there's an economic side to it. So, as long as they behave theirselves, I'm not antagonistic towards them. I can't say I like the look of 'em, but there you are. You do get used to them. Some people tell me: "I don't know how can you live next to all them old caravans". "Well", I say, "it all depends what you're looking at". We couldn't do without 'em and that's a fact. And you can look out from the jail, as the fellow says, and you can see mud or you can see stars.

I happen to be one of those chaps that have kept the habit on, of talking in the Gower way. When I was a boy, you'd hear all the old people talking like that. Since that time I suppose we've been 'educated' out of it. Funny thing, I didn't realise it till I went to work in Pembroke Dock. They had a dialect of their own down there, but I had no difficulty with that, because I found a lot of the words was the same, and not only the words, but there's a bit of a tune to it, you know, a lilt . . . "Why ay," they'd say, when in Gower we'd say "Mind thee" and things like that. No doubt a lot of our language came from South Pembrokeshire, p'rhaps the weavers come too, there was a lot of weavers here for a small area, mind. My grandfather was Will the Weaver. But most of the Tuckers come from Cornwall, as far as I can make out, way back.

I still like to turn to the old talk when I get half a chance. Very little left now, though. I used to like meeting Johnny the Lane of Llangenny, and he'd start: "Where't gwain, boy?" "Mind thee own business," I'd say, "Why should I tell thee?" "How art, boy? How'rt kippin?" and we'd carry on like that, quite naturally. Johnny had a turkey once that was bad, "A was a good turkey, mind thee", a said, "up to twenty pound or more". And a neighbour told him: "Tak'n into cold storage, boy, they'll kip'n for thee there till Christmas". "They can't do that, boy", said Johnny. But anyway, after a lot of persuasion he killed the old turkey, rough-plucked 'n and tuck'n into cold storage. And when a went back for 'n at Christmas, there was the turkey, stiff as a board, of course. A tuck'n home, and later his neighbour said to 'n: "Well, hast had the turkey, boy?" "Ay, ay. I had the turkey". "Well, what was a like?" "Oh . . . boy, twas all right, but mind thee, boy, twas blue wi' the cold!"

Mind you, Johnny's father was very dry, too. And his grandfather. Very old-fashioned. The story goes that Johnny's father went for a trip across to Ilfracombe, and the weather turned bad, so that the boat couldn't leave to come home. And Johnny's grandfather said to his wife: "'Tis pretty rough, maid", a said, "I think I'll light the lantern and go down and see if I can see 'n." "What's the good of going down with a lantern?", she said to 'n, "The blooming boat's over in Devon". "Ah," a said, "but mind't thee the wind is dead out here, Rhossili Bay, that's where a'll come in with this wind." And he insisted on going down to Rhossili Bay with his lantern, expecting the boat to come ashore there.

No, talking to people from different parts of the country, as I do, I find that wherever I go in the West Country they think I'm from there, Somerset, or Devonshire, or even Herefordshire. I was in a Herefordshire village some years ago, went up for some apples we did, and we went with a cousin to a bit of a social, country place it was, just like here. And I got chatting in the course of the evening, I believe I even sung to 'em, but they all thought I come almost from the next village, they could understand the lot. Then I remember, when I was a boy, a Cornish chap and girl came to work at one of the big houses here, they had funny ways and funny sayings, you could hardly understand them, but they were using lots of our words "thee casn't do this and that" "thee shust be here", just like we did, and they were young people, and in the kitchen they knew about the way we baked, with the brick oven and the bakestone, the 'plank' we called it, and the maid was quite at home. And they used 'pentan' for hob, too, but that's Welsh, isn't it? As I say, we must be proper mongrels. We can't belong to anybody really, can we? But it makes us different, though, doesn't it?

Swansea National Eisteddfod 1964. George Tucker (extreme left).

PART III

Farming

JACK RICHARDS

Dairy Farmer
Born in Rhossili 1896

My family had a small farm here—fifteen acres, as well as the Post Office and what they call the Lower Shop,—only two there are. It didn't look at first as if I would become a farmer, I hated things like gardening for a start when I was in school. That was my grandfather's fault. He was living on the hill, in Windy Walls, and he was terrible fond of gardening. But he couldn't walk except with two sticks, so he would dig his patch with a long-handled shovel during the day, then in the evenings I used to have to plant things for him (and then pick them) in the evenings after school. He'd grow seed potatoes and onions, and I'd have to wheel the blooming things down to the Lower Shop in a wheelbarrow, to sell them. So when other people were out enjoying themselves, I was kept busy. I've hated gardening ever since.

Then I went to the grammar school at Gowerton. Written and oral exams then, for a scholarship; and I come out top. I was the first child to go from the village to the grammar school in 1908. The school was 15 miles away so of course I had to lodge in Gowerton all the week. Nothing but horse-buses then. The house I lodged in was a long way from the school, I had to walk three miles to get there. Why so far I've no idea. But I can tell you, by the time I got 'home' there wasn't much work left in me, and of course there was no one to keep my nose to the grindstone. We were lodging with a widow, and she had two or three other fellows, colliery men, lodging besides. So there was no quiet at all in the house. My grannie wanted me to be a vet, and the family were very keen, but my father had bought another small farm, my brothers were quite a bit younger than me, and in the end I was quite glad to leave school and get into farming.

One of the jobs I had to do then was walk the sheep and cattle into town, for the butcher. By the time you got to Parkmill, or Killay Station, you'd be pretty glad to meet a drover who'd take over. By now they'd be getting pretty stiff, and a fresh voice and

Jack Richards with his grandmother standing at the door of Lower Shop, Middleton, Rhossili, 1908.

a different dog would work wonders. You had to watch cattle though. They'd go like mad for the first mile or so, then 'twas a dawdling walk, you'd hardly do two or three miles in an hour. And you daren't let them stop moving, if they once lie down, that's absolutely fatal. Sheep, too. But they weren't so bad once you got them away from home, and if you had a tidy dog. They would follow a strange road only when you've passed the familiar cliff lanes, and the ways up to the hill. They'd be along those like a shot. But sheep would stick together, that's something.

I got a farm of my own when I married. We took over a small farm near the middle of the village on valuation, one or two cows, a horse or two, that's about all it had. So we bought a couple of cows, and sold the milk. We had a few vegetables too, but gradually we grew into cows. For years then we sold milk in a fairly primitive way, people would come to the door with their can or jug and that was that. There was no cooling of the milk or anything. We made a bit of butter and gave the skimmed milk to the calves. After a while we got a cooler, but it was ages before we got a milking machine. My wife was a good milker, but she was dead against a machine. She felt it would be too much work in washing it out in hot water. After all, we still had to carry water, and hot water was a problem. And some dairy mistress she'd been listening to—some woman who'd been in college years before and hadn't changed—she said that it didn't pay unless you had twenty or thirty cows. In the end she gave in and threatened to finish with the dairy. But of course curiosity killed the cat, and she thought she'd better get the hang of it. So that was that. We were modernised!

But then regulations came in a bit keener, and we had to spend a bit of money. Up to then each farm could supply his neighbour with milk, but then they stopped you selling around unless your stalls were up-to-date. We were only tenant farmers, you see, and the estate wouldn't spend any money on us, the rents were so low, so the old buildings wouldn't pass muster, and before we could go any further we had to spend a lot of money on new buildings. We were the only milk retailers in the village after that, and still are. We sell milk to everyone now, farmers included. They don't bother with providing their own milk any more. What we don't sell retail, which is not much in winter, we sell wholesale.

Time went on and regulations got stiffer and tighter all the time. If you retailed milk you now got a Food and Drugs inspector coming to take samples, and inspect the stalls. Cleanliness they were after, there was no talk yet about TB in the milk. The Milk Marketing Board came in then and it turned out to be the best thing that happened for the dairy farmer. At the beginning the dairymen tried to kill it, they were making more profit on their own, on the side, too, a lot of it. We were selling to one fellow in Swansea, and he was crooked, we found, very greasy indeed. If he couldn't sell your milk he'd keep it a few days and send it back, complaining that it was sour. Then he'd cheat the Government on the levy they'd be taking, so much per gallon of milk. Say I sent him 500 gallons in a month. He'd put down 400 or 350 gallons in his declaration, and pay you the rest in cash. And he'd tell us the Board didn't know what it was doing. ''Let me fill your forms up for you'', he'd say, ''and save you the bother''. But I happened to know he was being watched, you see, so I didn't fall for his tricks. Anyway in the end he had to sell his farm to pay the fine on what he had swindled from the Board. Several others got stung too. In those days, before the war, the bus company used to run a van to carry parcels and milk in town. Then came the Milk Marketing Board lorries, we were all directed where to send our milk, and we were fixed up with a fellow who was as straight as the other one was a twister. Our farm had extra supervision because we provided the school milk.

We've always sold untreated milk. Only a farmer can sell milk that's not been pasteurised. A dairyman can't. But if it's untreated the cows have to pass tests for TB and brucellosis. When the testing started, it was optional, you could have it done privately, at your own expense, then if you were declared clear twice, you got a penny or tuppence more per gallon for it. And if you had any cows that reacted, you could sell these in the market. Then the tests became compulsory, and everything that failed had to be slaughtered.

I think now that untreated milk makes up only one per cent of the milk sold in the country, but I believe that it is far better if it comes straight and fresh from the farm. Otherwise it'll be tossed and swirled about in a lorry and it'll be a couple of days old at least before it comes to you. And if you pasteurise milk, you kill a lot of the good in it while getting rid of anything bad. I used to find that pasteurised milk had a definite tang on it and I didn't like it. But then maybe I'm prejudiced.

We eventually worked up to a pedigree herd, seventeen Friesians. I like a herd all the same, they look nicer. And Friesians are easier to buy. A shorthorn can look attractive, have a very big bag, but be very fleshy. A pedigree herd means a steady line, if you're breeding, but it has a few problems. For instance, they can never be allowed to drink from a pond in a field, only clean water is good enough for them. Very interesting, though—working up to a pedigree. You have a Herd Book, you see, all our cows had the forename Thurba, and in this book we had to keep details of every cow, and draw in the markings of all the calves, sketch them in the outlines provided, so that they can be recognised at any time in their lives.

Haymaking in the fields, early 1930s.

It was while we were building up this pedigree herd that we had a disaster, a real sweep-out. A long time after we'd been attested, too. We didn't have any fail when this was done, but the very next test we went all to pieces. Traces of TB were found in seven or eight of our cows. We'd not long bought one cow, as it happened, a good cow, too, poured out milk, but I'd never had a good calf from her. Anyway, the ministry man came, the cows were in and they looked a picture of health, shining like anything, but as he walked out through the stall he said, ''I'm afraid all these'll have to go. They all look in full bloom, except for this one here and she's infecting the lot . . .'' ''But she passed the test'', I said. ''Still, 'tis no good for you to leave her here'', I said, ''you'd better take her''. But the law was you see that you can't take a cow away if she's passed the test. Eventually, after I had undertaken to accept responsibility, permission was given from the Ministry to have her destroyed. It was very tricky, because if she were taken away and she were all right I could have claimed the full value for her. Anyway, we agreed a price and away she went. She was rotten all right. Must have been a bit of a throw-back, I should think.

If that sort of thing happens, it hits you hard. You lose heavily to start with. You can't replace the cows for the money they give you. And for three or four months you are without any income, because the whole place has to be cleaned out and disinfected. Our buildings were mostly concrete, luckily, so they could be scrubbed, not like wood. Still, if that fellow hadn't been so observant . . .

RUTH RICHARDS

Farmer's Wife
Born in Rhossili 1898

Someone who made a real mark on the life of the village, and on me, too, when I was a girl, was Miss Edwards, the school-mistress. She was the daughter of a minister and my word she must have been a personality, pretty advanced in her ideas, too, for the time. She always spoke Welsh at home and she tried to teach us a bit of Welsh in school, but in this part of Gower that was a hopeless task. I think she'd have been a Welsh National-alist if she were here today. She took a real interest in the people of the village and it was she made us aware of what we were to do and what we shouldn't, sort of taught us etiquette and good behaviour. The parson she wouldn't let near the school; the School Board had finished then, and she took it on herself to teach us how to behave to each other. I can remember her say-ing to us: ''Mind, if I'm down in the village during the holidays, that I don't see any of you girls out with your hair in curlers or in plaits. The place for that is in the bedroom''. And that has stuck with me ever since. You know, even now I can hardly come through my bedroom door before I comb my hair and wash myself. She used to take us for nature walks, the first we'd ever had. And especially she kept a check on the way we talked. She wouldn't allow any slang or swear words in or out of school. To tell you the truth, I never heard any slang or bad language used in our house when we were children. If any child spoke in Gower dialect or used Gower words she was onto it. Of course nowadays it's rather encouraged, but there was a lot of very broad dialect when she came here. You had to be careful when she was around . . . It so happened that I wasn't so rough as the others, so I became her pet pupil, I should think. I used to mark the work of the lower classes instead of going out to play. She wanted me to try the scholarship for the grammar school, but mother wouldn't hear of it, she really couldn't afford it. I haven't regretted it, because if I had I might not have married the man I did.

The choice of men was pretty limited in those days, as you can imagine. You usually went with one of the men of the village, or the chapel, or one of the 'cottage boys' perhaps. My sister married one of the cottage boys . . . as we called them. These were some of the first regular visitors we used to get down here. A few cottages would be let out, very few in those days, and a bunch of boys—with a man in charge—he may have been a teacher—used to come down on bikes to spend the weekend. They used to like to go around the cow-stalls and that, go out with a gun, that was their delight, and some of them were not short of money. In fact, one of them paid my father's expenses in a nursing home for six months before he died. Funny thing he never came to the village again. But he said to my mother ''If you need any more help, you come to me''. That was the type.

But I married a farmer's son and we moved into a farm of our own. We've been together now for going on sixty years. I remember well the first time I went out with him. It was I who asked him, because you see he was always the quiet one. He was always with his father and mother. He was never allowed to run wild. He was never allowed on the Bank. As far as that goes we got in trouble ourselves if we were found there, we'd get into too rough a company there, learn bad ways and bad language there, you see. So we didn't meet on the Bank, but at a Sunday School Christmas Tea—we always went round in a gang, we girls, had lots of fun together, and I said to this boy, ''Come on, you've got to take me home tonight''. No . . . there was nothing doing. At first anyway. But he did take me home. And after that I honestly couldn't get rid of him. I was going with G.M. at the time, having a great time, too. He'd take me into town, to the Empire Theatre, and that's why I went with him really. Oh, I was naughty. But anyway, I had to give up G.M. pretty soon, and that was the beginning of the end, like. After that I definitely couldn't get rid of him. I sometimes said to my mother, coming out of chapel . . . ''Look, mother, I'm coming home with you tonight, I know both my boys will be outside, and there's sure to be a fight. So I'd better come with you''. His family seat was near the front, a pew with a box for the hymn books, but he'd post himself in a seat near the back. And I'd ignore him. Oh, I used to tease him. He thought he'd catch me quicker by sitting at the back. And he did in the end. I've never been sorry, I must say, never.

NORMAN TUCKER

A Son of the Limestone
Born in Horton 1900

I'm the sixth generation of the Tucker family at our farm. Over three hundred and fifty years we've been here. My son is in charge now, and he's got a son, I'm glad to say, so . . . You see the first Tucker came to Penrice with one of the Mansel families back in 1609, from Watchet in Somerset, as a still-room boy to the squire. Followed him here on horseback. And he worked, I suppose, until he felt he wanted a place of his own, and this farm come free. A cottage it was then, of course. My father told me that he married one of the Clarkes from Oxwich. He'd been courting her, you see, and he went along now to ask the family for her hand, and the old man told him: ''Ay, thee canst have her for fifty pound and a pig''. And a picked up his hat and walked out, ''No thanks'' a said, ''I bean't buying any maid''. Anyway, not long after a message came over for him from her father: ''Thee canst have her for nothing, boy, she's pining''. So that's where we all came from. I believe we must be the oldest family in Gower. The old farmhouse was thatched. It was in the present rickyard, actually. Very expensive it got to keep, in father's time. So he asked the Estate to build him a new house. But father had to haul the limestone from the quarry himself and the sand from the beach and the timber from Swansea. Still, within a year he was sleeping in it. The Estate would do things for father because he was the oldest tenant, you see. And father . . . well it went through me a bit I must say. I was walking along the road with him one day, I was only a small boy, and the Estate's agent, Pritchard, came down on his horse, and as he came closer father took his hat off and stood almost to attention. I said to father: "Why do you do that? Mr George the school master tells us you only take your hat off to a lady". And he boxed my ear, "Don't be cheeky", he said and stood there with his hat in hand. Good riddance to Pritchard and all that I say . . .

I don't suppose things changed very much in the 300 years or so, one generation after the other, the farm was worked the same way right up to the end of father's days, well, until the tractors came. Ploughing the fields, working them with the horse and sowing, that was it. Same old timetable. I remember two things my father was rigid about. One was the planting of oats. Oh, he was very cross if we didn't have a field ready for oats by the 15th of March. Nothing was allowed to hinder that. For he used to sow the oats by hand on the 15th of March. Once he had that field sown he didn't mind about the rest. Except for the mangels. They had to be put in on the 7th of May. That was the date of the Sunday School Anniversary, too, so after dibbing the mangels in, by hand, the men and women would all go to the tea-meeting in Pitton. Oh ay, father was very fussy about those two dates. He used some of the old types of carts, too . . . the wain (we called it a ween), which had sides to it, and the truckle car, the narrow cart with two small wheels and without sides, and it had to be narrow to go through our lanes. I heard of the sleigh car, too, you dragged that along the ground, but I can't remember seeing one.

One thing that's been passed on in our family is a strong religious streak. We've all kept the chapel going in our time, and most of my ancestors were preachers. Two of them, two brothers, built the Methodist chapel here in our rickyard. One of them was blind, and he had a stile made behind the chapel so that he could find his way there from the house on his own. My grandfather, he was a local preacher, and his brother gave the land for a Methodist chapel at Oystermouth. My grandfather was well-known for a sermon he preached on Temperance Sunday. "Don't do as I do", he said, "do as I tell you. As a Methodist you mustn't take strong drink. I do take a nip of whisky now and again, but I always put a bit of salt in it . . .!

William Tucker, 1773-1853, builder of Horton Chapel.

Then a cousin of his, Charles Tucker, he became a missionary out in Fiji. The white man who went before him was too fat, so father told me, and they ate him, they tried to fatten Charles but failed, so they let him go free. Anyway, he came back alive and in 1842 he was in charge of a church in Bristol. They say that is why the Welsh hymn tune "Calon Lân" is well-known in Fiji, I don't know . . .

I suppose you could say that we always used to be poor, never had much money anyway. But we didn't seem to need a lot to live on. Times were bad but we always had a good table. We'd kill a lamb, and mother was wonderful with poultry, we'd have a duck or a goose,—we lived pretty well. My father never used a bank until 1920, and that was only after a robbery at the village shop. He used to keep all he had in a secret compartment in the bureau. Then there was Tom Jenkins, he was father's man, great chap, he worked for father for thirty-five years, and up to the war he never had more than 10/- a week. His wife took a few holiday-makers in, reared up six children, and when he died Tom left £800, not bad going, was it? It was ten times what I had at the time. Yes, for thirty-five years Tom walked the two miles to us here and he was in the stables by six every morning. And he took as much interest in the farm as if it was his own. Of course father treated him well, gave him potato ground, look, and enough mangels to keep his sheep through the winter; then he'd be able to snare a few rabbits, never needed to buy much at all.

Of course, a generation before that it was the barter system anyway. You took a pig to town and came back with stuff to eat. When father was a young man he used to go to Swansea every other Saturday, with two horses, ride one and load a sack of barley or wheat on each side of the other one. Then came the time when people began to want money. It might have been the Estate that started it. They'd give you money for your plot of ground and then charge you a nominal rent for it, like a shilling a year. But when a farmer died and his son followed him, the rent would rise, you see. Very keen on rents they became. Not a lot, but going up with each generation. That's why they didn't say anything if you enclosed a bit of the common. It became your land, and the more you enclosed the more you paid on rent. Then Pritchard had a mighty craze later on; he'd take a few acres off a farm before the next tenant took it over. Then he could charge as much as £2 an acre, you see. I was afraid of that myself. Father had been a tenant for 53 years and 10/- an acre was all he paid. But when he was ill in bed with cancer, I said to him: "The way things are going Pritchard will do that to us before I get a chance. I don't want you to give up, but I'd like to come in as a partner with you; you'll still be boss, but I can have some hold on the place when the time comes".

Anyway, things were all to pieces in farming after the war and I was very near to emigrating to New Zealand. A cousin of mine who'd gone out was trying to tell me what a wonderful place it was and all that. But I had promised mother and father I'd stay while they were alive. Anyway, Pritchard told me he wanted to raise the rent, not take any land away. But the rent was to rise double. In the end Lady Blytheswood stepped in, I will say that for her, and because father was the oldest tenant, she over-ruled Pritchard and got him to write out an agreement with me to pay the same rent as father had paid.

Here at one time, if you didn't farm, it was quarrying or oyster dredging. In father's day there were twenty-five locally-owned skiffs in the bay, and when the oysters were in season, these would take them up to Bristol and places. A few traces of the beds are still there, but all gone foul now. Then it was quarrying when the oysters were out of season. A number of quarrymen used to rent fields on our farm, and these fields took the names of these fellows and they've been known by these names ever since. They all had horses, to drag the limestone down into the sea at half-tide, then the boats would come in alongside the piles of stones, and the women would do the loading, standing up to their middles in the sea. So to get fodder for the horses they'd rent a field and work in pairs. Say they'd cut your field to hay this year and graze mine. Well next year I'd cut mine to hay and graze yours, you see? Then they'd make the hay up into cocks—lost art today—and they'd stick one of them long purple flowers, a foxglove, they'd stick one in every second cock, for you to know yours and me to know mine. They wouldn't divide a field in half, because there might be better grass in one half than the other.

Anyway, that's how a number of our fields got their unusual names. There's a Baker's Park, then a Thorkland, and a Cunniger, they must have got that one out of some dictionary. Betsy's Park is easy, that was the old maid who used to live there. And near to the house one is called Pound Close, because there used to be a pound there—for donkeys. Everyone in the village then kept a donkey, to carry wheat to the Mill at Penrice and water from Chapel Mere and things—and with these steep lanes you needed a lot of help.

I learned a lot from father. He was quite a well-read man, though he left school at eight, after three years in three little village schools. By eleven he was head ploughman.

Father's brother was master of a four-masted barque going round the Horn when he was twenty-eight. At that time there was fourteen captains living in Horton. All Cape Horners. Most of them were lost at sea.

WILFRED BEYNON

Sheep Farmer
Born in Rhossili 1902

Feelings aren't so deep about it now as they used to be, but we're always conscious in Rhossili of belonging either to Middleton, or Pitton, or Rhossili, the bit around the church. The different parts of the parish used to be like foreign countries. I remember one farmer living out the other end (Rhossili), and he was very fond of a girl there. Anyway, some fellow in Middleton started going after this maid, and the other boy was very annoyed: "Tisn't fair", a said, "Rhossili girls are for Rhossili boys, and Middleton the same, that's in the circle . . ." That was narrowing it down a bit, I should think. And now village people are marrying all over the world. But in those days we were absolutely isolated. There was a story of Sam Bevan, he could read, and he was the legal advisor. Well he was taking a neighbour farmer to Carmarthen to swear a will, and travelling along the other side of the Burry Estuary, they could see our hill here across the water. And Sam turned to this fellow and said: "I know a farmer over there", a said, "he goes to Neath and buys lambs for 5 shilling apiece, boy, then he takes them home and puts them up on that hill and before they're three-year old wethers, he sells them—big fat sheep". "Boy, I wish I was farming there", the fellow replied—and it was about him that Sam was talking! He had no idea where he was. I mean, how can you visualise that now? Pretty small world we lived in then. And now we can find our way all over the wide world.

My father had a small farm, with most of the fields on the beach—thirty feet above it really, with the big bay below. They were originally glebe lands and he rented them from the parson. We've always farmed the bay. There we've got the advantage of the sandy soil and we can get in the ground early to put the crops in. But then we've got disadvantages too. The salt winds there are cruel sometimes, and we have to manure those fields a lot. And then, where the sea swirls into this corner of the bay we've always got to watch out for erosion,—boundary posts keep getting washed away. Years ago there were banks of sand with marram grass and sedge as high as this house, with rabbits and all that. Then comes a spell of tremendously high tides, and it all gets swept away. Down to a narrow strip. Then after four or five years it'll build up again. Goes in cycles, but inch by inch that sea is pinching my land.

Of course, every farmer in those early days lived very simple. He'd put a few cabbages in the field with the mangels and a few cabbages in the field with the swedes. He'd grow the wheat, get the flour ground and bake the bread. They'd kill a pig and that was about all. They just lived off the land. They might sell a bullock or two, that'd pay for the rent and a few clothes, but it was just a case of living from hand to mouth. I have no recollection of being poor, or actually being hungry, but it was a near thing. We moved down to the Ship Inn about 1906, when it was closed as a pub. This gave us a few more fields. And father bought one field, the only one in the parish belonging to Lady Lyons. Don't ask me how she came by it; it's known as Clerks land. P'rhaps she bought it or won it in a gamble! We grew an acre and a half of potatoes there and we had some sheep of course. Father used to sell potatoes in Swansea, with a horse and cart. But during the First World War he had to stop that, because our horse was commandeered for the Army. After that we had to rely on market gardeners in Bishopston, near Swansea. They used to come down and go round buying up our potatoes.

The war gave things a bit of a lift because we could sell more, and prices were up. But then came the slump of 1921. That really hit everyone. But it meant we had to sell more cash-crops. A few carrots, a few cabbages,—a hard job, it really was a tough time. Because, you see, we were trying to break into new ways we knew nothing about. We didn't know about growing cabbage. What sorts to grow, how to get good crops, we were absolutely lost and isolated. At the same time we were competing in a market in Swansea with supplies from better growers, and the wholesaler didn't have much faith in us then. He'd ask himself, "If I drop my Evesham man will this fellow in Gower be able to deliver the goods?" That's what we were up against. We were not used to this competition. We had to show we were determined to supply him. I mean, in the farming we'd done before, if it rained all day, you just fed the stock and that was that. But now, if you had to cut cabbage on Wednesday to get them into Swansea on Thursday, you just had to cut them on Wednesday, whatever the circumstances. You wouldn't get the chance again. At this time, too, the growers nearer Swansea were getting poorer crops, because the stables were not so numerous. Lorries were coming in, and you can't get manure from lorries! So they found, because we had fresh ground and still plenty of manure, that our crops were now better, so they'd sell our stuff again. They gave us what we'd get from the wholesaler, so it was quite a bit of help to us. We started to get going then, with a bit more cash available. The stock numbers went up, and one thing helped the other.

With the Second World War of course everyone was flat out in production. In 1940/1 everyone in the village, except one, sold all his sheep. Because now we were intensifying the farming, growing to sell, and we had a market that would take anything we could supply. You can imagine, we had the Americans here in their camp, then prisoners-of-war, displaced persons, and that. If you even threw them cabbage leaves they'd be glad to eat them! We had one nasty scare of course. We were going to be evacuated! The whole of West Gower was to be cleared all out for military exercises. Nobody asked us about it. The plan was put to us in a public meeting, all cut and dried. But I'd heard before from a big Swansea businessman that he'd had a questionnaire about what would be the effect on Swansea if Gower was cut off? And he said, that the whole area would lose a valuable source of food. Anyway, in the end we didn't go. They went to Devonshire instead, I believe. It really would have been disastrous, though. Think of it! Where would we be now? Anyway, once the war was over, we had to try to get back to the standards of growing we had reached eight years earlier. By then Swansea market really was open to us, and once we could build up to quality crops, there was no problem to sell.

Of course, with my family, and I've had seven sons, only one with me now, sheep have been a constant. I know sheep, they were my training. Once I used to be a dab hand at counting them

—and I don't mean the old gag about counting their legs and dividing them by four! No, if they're running through a gap two or three at a time, I can count them as fast as they come, not 1-2-3, like, but 1-4-6-9 sort of thing. At least, I could! There used to be an annual sheep sale here, right outside this door—three to four hundred sheep and it attracted farmers from everywhere because this is a good place for sheep; they were always healthy, and didn't have liver fluke. There was a fair bit of liver fluke in North Gower, where that there bunch of land is on the estuary —the ewes would do well, have lambs, feed them, but they had to be sold fast after that, because they'd soon go downhill whereas ours didn't. With the coming of lorries it became easier to deal at Gowerton mart, where we go now.

I think a lot about the marketing of stock,—and produce for that matter. My father was interested in a dead-weight system for stock in the twenties, but that finished when the weighbridge come in. They used to guess the weight of a sheep, say, and then sell it dead-weight. For instance, if a sheep weighs 61 pounds, that's live weight. To estimate the dead-weight, you divide by 2, that's 30½, so the dealer will probably estimate it at 29 pounds, and sell it among the 29s. I've been a member of the FMC—that's the Fat Stock Marketing Corporation—for years, and I believe we should sell our stuff all dead weight. But you'll never get 100% co-operation from farmers. They're all individuals, they like their freedom of choice. That's why we haven't progressed so far in co-ops as they have in Europe. A case in point—in the last years we've had a sort of organisation called the Gower Growers of Early Potatoes. We got together, appointed a secretary, treasurer and that, and this was to handle our potatoes. But what happens? For about twenty years now the wholesalers in Swansea have got into the habit of ringing one of us up: "Can you get two tons by one o'clock on Monday?" They'd pick up the load, and the potatoes would be gone, to heaven knows where. I've done this myself,—had to. I've sold potatoes to Manchester, to Bradford, to Cardiff, Newport, Merthyr, up the valleys. Off the Swansea market, so it's not producing a glut here. But you see, the whole idea of a co-op is broken like this. The Milk Marketing Board had the right idea, I think. We had to sell to the Board, by law. But take stock, that's a free market if you like. I took some lambs to the market last Tuesday and I sold them well. I was very satisfied. Took some more up this Tuesday, and what did I find? Everybody had had such a good day the week before there was a glut—120 more lambs there! Prices down, of course. I believe with some channelling, some organisation, you could save a lot of wasted effort. I've always maintained that whether it be potatoes, lambs or cabbages the main thing is to sell at a reasonable price. Farmers should put all their efforts into producing and growing, not bargaining,—that should be out of our hands. As it was in war time, really. But human nature being what it is . . .

Similar sort of thing happens in the handling of sheep these days. Time was we used to have a compulsory dip for sheep scab. So some people would dodge it if they could. The police would supervise it, you see, and some farmers would say, oh we'll dip on Gower Show Day. They knew that the police are up to their eyes on that day,—so the sheep never got dipped. In the 1950s they stopped making it compulsory, sheep scab had been eradicated. But it's appeared again in the Midlands, I see. Very nasty thing. It means that you've got to double-dip now and lime out all the stalls and walls, heck of a job . . .

When you are grazing the hill and the clifflands you can't do better than Welsh Mountain, I reckon. Father bought some, fifty years ago, and that's still 70% of our stock. We do cross a bit with Cheviot now and again, to get size, but we daren't do much of it, the larger sheep are terrors to get over the walls and hedges, so we just get a splash of them, that's enough. We've always had some sheep over on Worms Head, got some there now. I swore I wouldn't years ago, after a bitter lesson I got, in 1932. We used to drive the sheep out to Worms Head, across the causeway when the tide was down. Then after a few months fetch them back. Now on the way out the incoming tide can be dangerous. The water can fill up behind you. No human being would be stupid enough to try of course, but one day, in the summer of 1932 a whole flock of my sheep decided to get out of their field and make their way over the causeway, when the tide was coming in. They got so far, then stopped. They couldn't turn back, it was too late; the water came up fast, and they were surrounded. That was the end. The currents are tremendous there, and the surge . . . anyway, I lost seventy sheep like that. If it hadn't been for a concert in the village hall, to help, we'd have been in a bad way. I don't know what it is, but once you put a sheep out on Worms Head, it can't be kept away from there. We had one old ewe had spent her whole life out there, couldn't keep her off. What we do now, we put lambs out on the Head, bring them back, fatten them a bit in the field, and get rid of them, sell them quick. Before the old urge can take them. Once they've had a taste of the grass out there, they'll never be safe again—that's a bit of family wisdom, now. We don't even risk putting them in a field on the cliffs now. Apart from that, rounding up our sheep is an easy matter, compared with Breconshire, say, where one chap has got a hill about six miles long and eleven miles wide. He's got a long day's job there. But he hasn't got the sea.

*   *   *

One thing about this village, I reckon, we've got the habit of thinking for ourselves. In our fathers' time there were beginnings of rebellious feelings against property and privilege. In the shape of the Penrice Estate, of course. I must say I didn't find the situation too bad. We were tied hand and foot, of course, you couldn't plough up an old meadow without asking permission. I remember in 1930, I thought I'd do this to grow more vegetables. So I put it to Pritchard the agent, and he said: "As long as you find the rent, damn it". That's all he was concerned about. The rent. And not a bad attitude, I thought. Some of the villagers were terrified of being turned out, but if you stood up to them . . . One time, after a rough night, a large chunk of plaster fell on one of the children's beds, a piece of the ceiling. No harm done. But I couldn't get the estate to be interested in repairing it. So I waited till rent day and I told the agent about it, and I asked him, "Now who'd be responsible if anything had happened to one of the children, you or me?" "Damn it", he said, "I've no idea—". "Well I'm going to find out", I said, and I walked out of the room. The next day he was here, with the builder. "Now", he said, "what can we do for you here?"

I doubt whether we'd have had a village hall if it hadn't been for the Estate. And that made a big difference to our life in the village. In my young days there was nothing for us, outside games. A parish meeting was a big event. And election meetings, well, it was something to go to, anyway. Nothing else of an evening for us. But once the hall was built, we could go in and light a fire and read a book or the papers or play draughts; it became a sort of club room. You see, the schoolmistress, Miss Edwards, had brought us up to think for ourselves. I reckon she did more for our generation than she or anyone realised. She believed in the Union Jack all right, but she instilled into us that every man is as good as his neighbour and has a right to his opinion, if he's got the talent. I suppose she also killed off a lot of the Gower dialect, by making us try to speak "proper English".

The break up of the Estate in the end was a good thing, for those who were in, as tenants. But of course, it's getting harder every year now for the small farmer. And where's a young man going to get the cash to start up on his own? Used to be that the merchants would give you credit. But not today. Only this week, we changed a tractor, bought a good reconditioned 165. Difference—£500. And the driver who delivered it wouldn't go until he'd got the cheque. How is a youngster going to start? If you buy stock, machinery, they expect the cash to be there, on the nail. And if a cheque bounces, they're down your throat. Being a landowner yourself is a mixed blessing.

I don't blame people turning to tourists now as a source of income. Even back in the twenties, when it started to become a supplement, I reckon it helped to raise the standard of living in the villages. And this would be a poor place today without the tourists, I'm sure of it. I know a lot of people make a lot of money out of it, too much perhaps, but money has a habit of rolling, and there's always the chance that it might roll your way. Some of it, anyway!

NORMAN RICHARDS

Farmer
Born at Kimley Moor 1902

I started with my father on the farm when I left school at fourteen. I learned a lot from him, I must say. He taught me to do a
job thoroughly. "Don't rush it", he'd say, "you can learn later on
to do it faster". Good advice, that was. At home we were lucky,
we always had plenty to eat. We had our own bread, and our own
butter, and I remember I often made a meal of just that. Compared with that butter you might just as well put cart grease on
your bread today. Cheese, too, my mother made mounds of it. I
can taste it now . . . honey-sweet it was. Bacon, plenty of eggs,—
we were as strong as horses. We were up at half past six, my
father's plan was to do the biggest half of the jobs before dinner.
Then we'd finish at five. I liked that, because I was able to be off
on my bike into the village to meet the boys on the Bank, and
play football, or quoits, or draughts, or do a bit of boxing. I was
never bored. If it was a bad night my brother and I would play
draughts at home, with the light of the oil lamp—how my
mother used to see to sew and mend I can't imagine. In the village we had some of the best quoits men in Gower, draughts
too, we won both the cups, and I was in the teams. I suppose I
played in every team that was ever picked in the village. I did
any amount of boxing, too. There were a lot of fellows mad on
boxing. We used to meet in an old milling parlour near here. I
was only a short little fellow, but whatever height the others
were, I could manage to put them under, usually. I did get a
proper bashing once, I remember. In fact I'll never forget it. But
he didn't catch me a second time.

But when I was twenty I lost an eye, and I really thought I'd
never play anything again. It happened while we were out with
the gun, ferreting rabbits. There was a wild sort of fellow with
us, a collier who used to come down to come out with us. If he
caught sight of a rabbit he'd get so excited he seemed to lose
control of everything. On this occasion he fired through the
hedge, and I was on the other side. He got the rabbit on the

bank, but the pellets come through to me. I've got them in me now, in my arm, in my side here, though they're gone pretty deep by now. Anyway, one at least went through this eye, right to the back of my skull. This happened in October, and do you know, by the following April I was playing quoits again. At first I could have sworn the quoit was landing on the peg when it was a good yard short. I was a long time getting the measure of it, but it came. With boxing it was easier, I'd take my glass eye out and take a chance with the good eye. I never bothered. I've had three glass eyes before this one, and this one is plastic, cost me eight guineas. Very natural, mind. The doctor was here with a student once, and he made him examine both my eyes, without telling him one was false. It fooled the student, anyway,—he was a long time trying to find the retina!

Then, as luck would have it, I developed a cataract on my good eye. I was ploughing in a field near the road one day, and I could see six sows in the next field, when I knew that we only had three, and later I saw a car coming along the road with another car on top of it—it was time then to have an operation. It was very successful, really, and I can see to read again, though I had to give up driving.

It didn't stop me using my gun, mind. And in the early days I shot plenty of pheasants—on the sly. We had to be very secretive about them. You see, the shoots from Penrice Castle used to cover the rough ground at the top end of our farm. In fact they usually had lunch at our house—the beaters would have beer and sandwiches in the barn, the toffs would come into the house. Then about four o'clock they'd pack up and go. And my father would say to me: "They've gone, boy, see what you can find". So I'd have a go at them, shoot scores of them, but I'd find some with broken wings or legs, unable to rise. If we'd been found out, we'd have had notice to quit, no doubt about it, that was the chance we took. One fellow living near us, he had to leave because he was caught poaching.

My father was a tremendous good shot, a terrible man for the gun, he was. I remember one incident during the First World War. I was about twelve and there was a Zeppelin passing, so quiet, like a big cigar, you know. And we were in the fields rabbitting, when I saw him lean down onto a bank and point his gun at this thing. I was scared stiff that he was going to fire at it, and bring it down! But I suppose it must have been at least two miles off . . .

Of all the jobs on the farm it was ploughing I liked best. I won lots of prizes at it, and it was I who showed a young farmer how to plough—well-known fellow now—when his father died and left him the farm. I took him to many a match. Mind, his father had been a good ploughman, perfect, I'd say. First thing I look for is a straight furrow, I don't like dog's hind legs. Then two furrows must never lie against each other, or show up in pairs, the rows must be closened neatly. It was much more interesting ploughing with horses, I mean, you can't talk to a tractor, can you? I always kept talking to my horses, and they'd turn around at the end of the row without my having to steer them. I'd just say ''Coom here about'', that meant turn left, and ''Gee-off'', for turn right, and the old horse would know it. Same with planting potatoes, in the old way. We used to plant in the open drills, at the bottom, then we'd use the horses to

Norman Richards at Gower Show, early 1930s.

close the rows. First of all both horses would walk on the spuds, then you'd get one of them to walk on top of the row, and that needed a bit of training, I can tell you. The best horse I had, if he'd put one foot down over the spud, I'd say "Up!", and he'd bring his foot up as if it had been stung by a bee! All training. It's all made very easy today, isn't it?

Harvesting with a combine, again, has made it all simple, but you don't have the corn we used to get with the steam engine and threshing machine. They used to clean it much better. We'd have first grade, for seed, seconds for the animals, and thirds, that would be nothing but a load of weeds and rubbish. Now the whole lot is all thrown in together. But it's all finished in two days, that's the thing.

I preferred ploughing with the horse, but I always used a tractor in a ploughing match, for one simple reason: my father wouldn't spend the money on the harness, and all the dressing-up that went with it. You know, the blackening and the polishing and the plaiting, and the brasses and the little bell on the top of the bridle. Mind you, they did look nice. I'd like to have had the prize for the neatest turn-out.

Winds are a problem on the moor here, north-west is very bleak, and we're very open to the weather. If you see a butt, a black line of cloud straight across the sky there, to the west, it's a sure sign of rain. And if you hear the dogs barking at the farm between us and the sea or hear them talking very plain, the same. We did try planting trees outside the house to shelter the dairy, but they didn't last long. Then in Festival of Britain year I helped Stephen Lee plant a sort of commemorative line of trees eastwards along the main road. You can see it now, though many of them failed, a few survived, I think the best one now is a Cornish elm, but they really catch it there. Not that we get winters like we used to years ago. I remember my father's moustache, I've seen him carrying the hay out to the cattle when it was snowing and freezing and he'd come back with icicles hanging from his moustache!

I can put up with the visitors if they don't bring their caravans with them. I don't like seeing them in the fields. But it must be quite a thrill for some of these people coming from the Midlands and places who've never seen the sea before. They think it's wonderful. Mind you, I've never done nothing with the sea myself, never liked it. I couldn't stick bathing, I'd shiver like a rat. I don't suppose I've been within a sight of a beach for over ten years, and it's not a mile from here! Same with Gower itself. Some people go mad about Gower, and its beauty. They think it's marvellous. But that's the funny thing. We can't see it ourselves, we're so used to it.

ERNEST RICHARDS

Agricultural Politician
Born in Rhossili 1907

Ours didn't have the same home atmosphere as other houses in the village. I lived in the Post Office, in Rhossili and my mother inevitably found herself a kind of Welfare Officer and Information Centre for the village. I remember, when there were a tremendous number of forms and things to be filled up relating to the census in 1911—I was only about three or four—and I used to listen to the conversation about these, no idea what it was about, of course. The house was hardly ever just the family, there was always somebody in and out. Even in the evenings the old men of the village used to come in for tobacco or bread and sit on the settle and yarn. And when the First World War started, there they'd be, fighting the battles and discussing the strategy, in a very knowledgeable way—all above my head of course, but it fascinated me. I've been a great listener ever since. After I went to bed I'd stay awake, listening to their conversation coming up through the floorboards. Then on Sunday mornings, my mother used to take down the official news bulletin on the telephone—we had the only telephone apart from the coastguard, that was a private one—then she'd write it out and stick it up outside, so that the old boys could read the latest. Everything sort of radiated from the Post Office.

There really wasn't much to do in the village in those days

except talk—and listen. I've always loved to hear people talking
—speeches, sermons, anything. We virtually had no newspaper
—daily papers only started during the war, when people were
anxious to know what was happening, it gave a tremendous
impetus to news-spreading. Even with us children, I remember
the scare among us as to whether our horses would be requisitioned. The farm horses were personal friends of ours, and
when father used to drive into Swansea on Wednesdays and Saturdays, we'd be anxious to see them come back, because we'd
heard the War Office was in the habit of rounding up suitable
horses for war work. My parents didn't seem to be worried, they
knew better, but we were very concerned whether our Fly
would be 'called up'.

   The little village school I went to had a good lot of books, so I
became an avid reader. My mother used to read to us, too, generally a serial story in a magazine. And I learned to read long
before I could understand the words,—I had to ask my mother
what it meant. But the all-pervading influence in our lives was
the chapel, twice on Sundays as well as Sunday School. I
enjoyed the sermons most of all. I used to vow that if they ever
stopped having sermons I'd never go again. I still feel like that.
As I say, I love to hear people talking, but over the years I've developed a kind of defence mechanism which helps me to switch
off if I find that what I'm listening to isn't worth hearing.

   I was very close as a child, and rather easily scared. I remember I broke my arm coming home from school, for the August
holidays. In those days a broken arm was not an everyday occur-
rence, and it was thought to be a terrible thing, among children
anyway. To me 'broken' meant 'broken off', and I was convinced it was going to fall off. Anyway, the doctor and nurse
came down, they made some splints from a chocolate box, with
a big carving knife, then they got me down on the floor, the
nurse knelt on me, they pulled the bones apart and set them
properly—a terrifying experience it was, and I had to have a bed
on the floor until it mended. An odd thing then, I started to
walk in my sleep. I used to dread going to bed. I didn't tell anyone, because I thought they'd tie me down. I just thought it was
the sort of thing you ought to keep to yourself. I'd heard about

one woman in the village who'd walked in her sleep, right through the bedroom window. Anyway, eventually the doctor called to say he was going to come down in a few days to open up the splints, and if it hadn't set straight, they'd have to break it again. I overheard this, and when he did call, I was missing. I'd run away, and they found me on Worms Head. My sleep-walking came to an end, but even when I went back to school the children wanted to know whether I had one hand or two! Nowadays a child thinks no more of it, they know all about hospitals and plaster and 'broken' limbs.

I'll tell you what helped me to learn things quickly as a child. We used to have a 'do' at the chapel every Tuesday for any soldier who was home on leave. There were thirty from the parish away in the war. And all the school children had to recite or sing, and the lad would get a small presentation. I had to learn a new poem for that every week. A different one from what we'd be doing at school, this became expected of me. It certainly gave me a love of poetry, I stuffed my head with it. And it is still my favourite reading. I've got a volume of Burns at my bedside at this moment. I can't understand all the dialect, but I love reading him. I've never written any real poetry myself, but I've often done a bit of doggerel now and again for a special occasion. There were rhymsters in every village in those days, commenting on the topical stuff going on at the time. I love doing this, even now. If there's anything like a presentation up at Agricultural House, where I spend a lot of my time these days, I generally knock out a verse or two. In fact, I've got one on me now, for a particular friend of mine who got married the other day. I put it on a wedding card I sent to him. He's the Secretary of the Parliamentary Department:

"From members of the Parliamentary Committee to its House of Commons Lobbyist and his bride:—

The ceremony's over now,
A new "House" today is born.
Your choice is made, your vows exchanged,
Your oath of allegiance sworn.

Forget today all G.D.O.s,
    (that's General Development Orders, he deals with those)
White Papers, blight, pollution.
Instead plan sessions by the score,
With no thought of dissolution.
May your Queen's Speech a blue-print be
For a life of sweet contentment;
May Bills be few and far between,
And Acts need no amendment.
May calm approach and cool debate,
Well spiced by humorous quips,
Produce consensus policies
And displace Three-Line Whips.
May you both ensure that reason's peace
Holds sway within your borders,
And raise more interesting things
Than fruitless Points of Order . . .''

For some odd reason, the war for me centred around the local
boy home on leave. It was the thing to do to invite him to tea,
and the fact that anyone had actually been over the sea to anywhere was a terrific thing to me.

My grandfather and grandmother were both very old, and
they were always in the house, so it gave me a long link back to
history and other wars. My grandmother used to talk about her
father who fought at Trafalgar. I've got his medal here now, his
Trafalgar medal. This was certainly out-of-the-ordinary run of
talk.

I couldn't leave school fast enough. Life seemed much more
attractive outside. We had a bit of land, and I lived in the open
air, though my memory of winters then is just a morass of mud.
Still, I was impatient to start working the horses. I used to enjoy
that. But in a way it was a serious gap in my growing life. I
didn't read a single solid book from the time I left school until I
got married. Ten years. Newspapers, yes, but never a book.
Then they started evening classes in the village—W.E.A. and
with them came a big change in my life. Professor Ernest
Hughes used to come and talk to us once a week, he used to

Ernest Richards with his grandmother, 1908.

have supper at our house. I was very attentive at these classes, on Current Affairs, and I got down to written work for one of the tutors. Soon he offered to recommend me for a scholarship to Oxford or Cambridge at the end of one session. But I wanted the knowledge without going to school, and I still thought that to plough and to sow and to reap and to mow was the life for me. I used to borrow the books recommended by the tutors at the classes, one of them was Strachey's "The Country's Struggle for Power", which became the most influential book in my life, and Tawney's three works. Anyway, this started me off, and I got hold of all the political books I could lay my hands on. Without these classes my life would have been very different indeed.

In the Autumn of 1922 I went to a Glamorgan Agricultural Course at Swansea University College. You had to be sixteen to go, but I was only fourteen, and told a lie on the entrance form. It lasted all that winter—four months, with a class of about 90 to 100. I did well there and in the exam at the end I got second prize. I suppose if I had been moving in a larger circle, this would have changed my life.

Twelve years later I became a farmer like everyone else, in Horton. Early potatoes had just been discovered. Gradually it was realised that Gower had special advantages of climate, and a new variety of early potatoes—Arran Pilot—gave us the impetus. This was a breakthrough. Up to then cropping had been poor, though Gower potatoes were very good to eat. An agricultural lecturer introduced us to the potato box idea, the chitting box, and this was the beginning of the early potato boom. The Second World War came, much more ploughing had to be done. I thoroughly enjoyed farming, I had an enormous feeling of satisfaction from the physical acts of ploughing and hedging, and of course working the horses. I think I lost some of my zest for that when the horses went, and mechanisation took over, inevitable as it was. It took the edge off for me. Besides this, two things had happened by the end of the war: I suffered a couple of quirks of health, and I had become interested in agricultural politics in a big way. As a member of the local N.F.U. I did a good bit around the country, explaining political situations in agriculture. Then I was put on a sub-committee deal-

ing with pests, and problems of national deferment and that
sort of thing. I became deputy to the county delegate going to
London, succeeded him when he retired, and that's how I'd
have gone on, with far less travelling than I do now. For quite an
odd thing happened. A representative from Wales was required
on the negotiating body of the Price Review. The Price Review
had by now become a statutory exercise every year, by a team of
brass hats from the N.F.U., most of whom lived in the eastern
part of Britain, with a different outlook on farming. There was a
move afoot to get someone from the western side, so there was
an election, and I got elected. Before that, it was a trip to London every second month for three days, as well as local and
branch work, meetings and so on. But once on the Price Review
team all this changed. It was an enormous exercise for an
amateur, a farmer, rather than a professional statistician, or an
economist. I now had a tremendous amount of paper work to
absorb, as well as the plenary sessions to attend: we'd assemble
in Whitehall at 9.30 a.m. or 10 a.m., go on till about 6 p.m., go
back to Agriculture House and have a big inquest on the session, then prepare for the following day. And that used to go on
for five weeks! The Civil Servants and our people would deal at
length with the present state of the industry and with particular
lines, say, beef, the record of last year, of imports, availability,
prices, prospects of supplies from the Argentine, New Zealand,
Australia, they'd know how many male calves, born two years
ago, would be coming to beef and so you'd build up a whole picture of the trends. Also there'd be the political prospects of tar-
iffs being raised in other countries against some of our products,
and any action we needed to take. Then there was the internal
state of the economy and so on. Then the Price Review would
start. After that you'd be about a month explaining it all to
farmers. You'd start in your own county, inevitably a row
would blow up, dire forecasts would be made, so you'd have to
go and explain the background, the difficulties and all that.

Well, once you start that sort of life it's like an avalanche, no
stopping it. At the same time I became vice-chairman of the
Parliamentary Committee; in 1965 I got into the chair, and I've
been there ever since. That meant the Price Review was only

part of the job. The change was very sudden for me. At first I found it mentally very hard and I often thought how much easier it'd be planting potatoes. But once I got a grasp, it was tremendously absorbing, it was impossible for me to resist enjoying it. I like to think that it isn't just a sense of power, or a feeling of superiority. It could be smugness, perhaps, thinking you know a bit more than the next man. But I like to think that because I've done what I've done, seen what I've seen, a lot of people understand their agriculture better. Explaining it to other people is my biggest satisfaction. I must admit, too, that I have enjoyed some political influence in the sense that Ministers of the Crown have understood the agricultural position better after hearing what I've had to say. Does that sound big-headed? I'm sure it's true.

If I wasn't a fairly alert political animal I don't think the life would have had the same attraction. I do feel that agricultural politics is a branch of other politics, and whatever Government is in power, you just have to face up to whoever's there.

I did have a chance to go further. There was a move to put me in for the Vice-chairmanship of the N.F.U. and I could have had it, with a wink from me. There were lots of speeches begging me to do this. But I firmly resisted it. And I know I did the right thing really. I'd have had to give up the chair of the Parliamentary Committee, and I couldn't have done it so well. You have to understudy the President, go around making pleasant noises at dinner parties and that, and generally be a bit of a dogsbody. You get hived off from the main stream of politics, and, let's face it, that's what I'm really interested in. How agriculture impinges on the main stream of politics, that was my abiding love, and still is now. I've tried never to separate myself from farming. I suppose, if I'd started twenty years earlier, I'd have gone into politics proper. I think politicians are great people, I won't listen to anyone who runs them down. Following the manifesto in the Queen's Speech, I have to meet these people and talk, very informally, to shape up political opinion as best one can—and you've really got to be factual, and what you say must be honest opinion and unvarnished by any desire to create effect or stir—or they'll soon take that with a pinch of

Last meeting of the Special Area Planning Committee. Ernest Richards, seated extreme left, and George Tucker, standing second from right.

salt and write you off. Glibness is useless. You really have to
have knowledge and convince people that you've made a deep
and balanced study of the subject.

What helps me a lot in this is the fact that whenever I can fit
in half an hour or so, I sit in on the select committees. I find one
that sounds interesting and I just slip in and sit at the back,
quietly, and see if I can fathom which way their minds work.
Sometimes I attend to questions far removed from farming, but I
find it all fascinating, the probing this way and that, in the
questioning and the answering. It's all part of my self-training. I
like to see what I can pick up, how the system works, what
makes it tick, what influences and pressures M.P.s are subject
to, and I find all this helps me to do my job better. When I am in
London, there are not many nights when I'm not at the House
of Commons. I'm well known to the police there. To many of
the M.P.s too. They come out and have a chat, and ask me
about something that's been puzzling them in some debate on
agriculture that is just finished. You'd find it a terrible bore if
you were not fascinated by it. It so happens I am.

All this has meant terrible time-pressures to keep in touch
with my home parish two hundred miles away every weekend,
but I hope it has not affected my relations with all those I
know there or in the county. I've perhaps been over-anxious in
a way to keep my local connections. I'm still a member of our
Parish Council, they'll hold the meetings at the weekends, to
suit me, and until lately I used to be very active on the Village
Hall Committee and the Gower Show. I've tried to keep in
touch even when I haven't had the time to do it.

As far as the development of farming in Gower is concerned,
there have been many factors. There's been more to it than
mechanisation. Nothing much had changed in these parts, you
see, until about 1926. Potato growing and mixed farming were
coming into their own by then, new varieties of grasses were
getting known, but people were only beginning to talk about
tractors. They didn't get here until about 1934. The other
important thing of course was the effect of the Depression and
it was 1936 before Government intervention was beginning to
give some sort of guarantee to farming. This sparked off lots of

changes. Farmers became surer of their future, they became land-hungry, whereas before land boundaries had stayed the same for generations. I don't think there was a land sale in Rhossili from the end of the First World War for about fifteen years. All from father to son. But once there was a degree of confidence, everyone was looking for a bit more land. The break-up of the Penrice estate meant that land became available for the first time. Mobility of labour was another thing. Lorries, cars, motor-bikes made all the difference. People could even go into Swansea to work. Before that a man could spend all his life on the same farm or in the same village.

Until the Second War there was no piped water supply, which meant that farmers couldn't produce milk. The change from livestock to milk took place in a big way in the 30s. After that it went full circle, and we went back to beef and sheep again.

The land on the whole is shallow, but it's very free-draining, so we're free of expensive drainage problems. In fact, the first time I came across drainage problems was when I went into the political field. The commons are now used more by ponies than by sheep. They live out in the open, wild, then they're sold for children's riding ponies, a fair number exported, and highly thought of. More highly than by motorists, I know. They create a terrible problem on the roads. I suppose a pony has a legal right to stray from one common to another, and so become a menace to traffic, in fact it is virtually impossible to catch a pony in an illegal position. And when you consider that about 14,000 acres of Gower is common land—about half the peninsula!

GEORGE BEYNON

Farm Worker-Retired
Born in Rhossili 1909

Tremendously hard work, farmwork in my time, but I loved it.
I wasn't all that strong as a youngster and I remember my
mother taking me to a specialist, and he said, ''Whatever you
do, Mrs Beynon, don't let him go on a farm''. ''I can't see how
that's possible'', she told him, ''that's all he thinks about''.
''Try to get him in an iron foundry or something''. But onto a
farm I went, straight from school. My wages to start with were
4s. 3d. a week, plus my food. Eventually it went up to 7s. 6d. a
week. But then my uncle took me to run his farm with him, at
Fernhill (Vernal we call it), just the two of us, 75 acres. He gave
me then 21s. a week, working all the hours that God gave. I got
married then and he gave me an extra shilling. ''Here you are'',
I said to my wife, ''this is for you, this is what you're worth!''
But the hours! Today, the boys do most of the graft sitting on
their bottoms. Take sowing manure. You drive your tractor
now, work your elevator, and that's all there is to it. We had to
pick every bit of it up, load it in a cart, haul it out to the field,
and then sow it, by hand.

We used to do a lot with horses, and feeding beef. We had
about a dozen animals for fattening. As long as my uncle had
something to sell in March, then again in September, he'd be all
right, he'd have enough to pay the rent. I remember my grandfather sold his last bullock to the butcher over the hill at 10s. a
score, that's 6d. a pound. I can see him now bringing the bullock out of the shed, and he said to my father: ''There thee art,
Johnny, this is the last rent I'll have to pay''. His farming days
were over. But my delight, then, and ever since, was a pair of
horses, good heavy horses, to feed them and follow them. Oh I
used to love them, and I had them so full of corn, you know. My
uncle used to say to me: ''I reckon thee ought to have a bicycle,
George, to keep up with them horses''. He was, you see, my
uncle, the last fellow who did the horse-bus. And he had to keep
them in good fettle to do the job. My grandfather before him

used to give the horses the same feed as the bullocks he was fattening for market. But my uncle had different views about that. He had to find the food, the money. For instance, he would notice the turkeys scratching among the horse manure in the stable, and then he twigged why: "Damn you, boy, you're still giving Captain and Polly extra corn". "Well, Uncle Jack", I told him, "'tis your work they're doing, I'm prepared to follow them however fast they go". The same pair used to haul the rocket (life-saving) apparatus, too, when it was called out; we had to shine up the whole outfit for that. Very smart they looked. Funny thing, Polly,—she was the older one,—all white, once she was spruced up and oiled, if you opened the door, she'd never fail to go straight to the rocket station, right across the village, no need for a word or a touch, she'd get on the road, turn left, then all the way, by herself. My grandfather used to tell of the time, too, when he had to take a special brake into Swansea, at 6 o'clock in the evening, it was at the time of the celebrations for George V's coronation. But the old horse didn't like it at all. No sooner was the brake hitched on than he turned sideways and went clean over a wall, everything with it. Then when they eventually got as far as the town it took three to lead him down in. It was dark by then you see—and he'd never seen lights in his life before. Always home by lighting-up time.

Then when the motor-bus started, in the twenties, my grandfather brought his two horses down and stood them on the Bank as Jim Brockie drove the first one through, and he said: "There it is, Captain and Polly, there's your saviour".

"How do you keep them in such good shape?" one of the village fellows asked me one day. "Well", I said, "I put their brush and comb in their manger". He was a bit puzzled but he went home and he tried it himself, he put their brush and comb in the manger, but nothing happened. He had missed my point, —there's no doubt, the secret is in their feed.

But you can keep your tractors. The point is this, you could talk to the horses, and they'd prick up their ears, and I reckon they understood practically everything I said. Great. Then again, the tractor couldn't tell you what time to finish, but with the old girl up there, come half past five and say we'd be at the end nearest the house, she'd stop, and not pull out or turn, but stop and wait. Look at your watch, half past five. You got so used to it. The old girl would need a bit of coaxing then.

I never was one to wander much. I could stay at home and I'm sure life was better and fuller than it is nowadays. You made your own enjoyment round your own little dingle, fishing, shooting, crabbing. Half a day, Saturday afternoon that's all you were allowed in town, if you wanted to go. "What art going for now, George? Pair of boots or what?" You'd have to have a good excuse. If you wanted to meet a girl, you had to walk miles. Across the hill to Llangennith was nothing. Then back to Kennexstone Cross, that was the meeting place for the villages. On a Sunday evening there'd be well over a hundred there, fellows and girls from all parts around. Though how I met Gwen (she's my second wife, you see), was this.

Gwen: "I was one of the first of the landgirls billetted on a Gower farm, in 1940. I really enjoyed it. I did everything, except ploughing. Cut the corn, rolled the fields, picked stones, raked, always with the horses, and the pigs. First thing in the morning there was milking, bedding, and cleaning out the stables. Very hard, especially in the wet. I did the gardening, too, everything the hard way. Then later I did the delivery of the milk. No bottles or cartons of course, just the can and the pint measure. And I had a hard slog to the ends of the village. And I was lucky if I had enough milk left for the house. All on foot. That's how we met. "Good morning, Mr Beynon", "Good morning, Gwen", so it went on every day for a long time. The next thing. "Good morning, George" . . ."

And that was the end of me!

In 1925 I went to a larger farm, and here I had a most marvellous boss, I'll say that. They had a lot of boys there, beginners, from the Homes many of them, and they had to be shown what to do, no disrespect, mind, they just hadn't had the experience. But the farm wasn't run in the business-like way it is today. As long as they made ends meet they were happy. I mean in my time I don't suppose there was 200 sheep on the farm, and in the autumn the best of the flock were sold, to get some money back. Now there's about 500 breeding ewes in the same place. I know for certain that on times there wasn't as much as £20 in the bank. Of course then a lot of things were done by barter. If you kept a pig, say, rather than have money for wages you might like a bit of barley for the pig, then for a day's planting and a day's picking, they would let you have all the potatoes in one row, when it was opened up. The manure, the seed, the working of the ground, the farmer saw to that, and he'd tell you, your row is such and such a number. It'd be all down in his book, and that would be in addition to your wages, not inclusive of them. That went on at every farm.

It was just after the War that talk of a Farmworkers' Union came to us. And the boys put me in a very awkward position. They were getting a bit agitated about the wages and the hours they were putting in. I was the oldest there so they turned to me. "You should do it, George", they were on to me. But I was quite happy with things as they were. So I pondered it over. Then one day we were having a mug of tea, and the boss was there. And he said to me: "What's up. George, you've gone very quiet these last few days?" I didn't say anything. "You know, I rather think there is something up," he said, "I want you to come out with it". So I told him, we were all there. "Right, boys," he said, "if that's what you feel, there'll be an increase in your wages from this week, and we'll finish at 12 on Saturday. Only I don't want to be on my own all the weekend". So it was fixed, we'd take it in turns to keep an eye on things—and never once did he check on us or ask what we were doing. And never did he book any overtime himself, he'd just ask you how many hours, and there was the money. No quibbling, ever. He was very good. Over thirty years I was at that farm and though I was away when my first wife was in hospital, I was never left without a day's wages. I had to retire early owing to ill health—I suppose I did too much, working all day and fishing all night—but the boss—I mean the son now—insisted we stayed on at the cottage and paid no rent or rates. "What we've got now you helped to make, George", he said. That didn't go on at every farm!

BOWEN RICHARDS

Cliff Farmer
Born in Rhossili 1912

I was fifteen when my father died, so I had no choice, I had to carry on the farm on my own. It was a small mixed farm—only 26 acres it was. So as a youngster of 16 I had to turn to doing all things, sowing corn even. By hand, of course. Lem Richards taught me how to do this: ''Throw it up well, boy, throw it up, it'll come down all right. If you don't it'll come up in streaks''. Some of our land ran along the edge of the cliff, the rest was on what is called the Vile.

The Vile is an area of 75 to 80 acres which is divided up into strips and way back it was shared out among all the farmers in the parish, a very ancient field system, it seems. Ten of us have land there now, one strip here, one there, very awkward to cultivate with modern techniques. Each strip is separated from the next one by a lansher (landshare), a narrow ridge of grass that tends to get poached away by the ploughs on either side. You've got to watch your neighbour carefully sometimes. We have been trying to bring together strips, but not with much success. If someone has a piece with rocks in it, no one wants to exchange it with him. At the same time, if you've got a good strip you are reluctant to let it go. In places the ground is very thin, two or three inches of soil at the most. The plough will bump over the rocks at one place, then sink down eight or nine inches at another. We're breaking shares all the time. So in a dry summer you can have corn up to your waist at one end, while at the other end it's all burned away. Where it has been possible to join strips, a bit of fencing is possible, so that we are able to graze some stock. But on the whole the ground has to be farmed for crops. A six-year rotation was quite usual: corn, followed by roots, then potatoes, with a one year ley. We'd plough it up, put grass seed down and give it a rest for a year. We'd get a crop of hay from it, then plough it up again.

We get the full force of the Atlantic gales on these cliffs, of course. But on the Vile, there is a fair bit of shelter from the dry-

stone walls all around. We didn't suffer from the sea-winds
until we started growing early potatoes. But on the cliff-top you
can't get away from them. There are times when you literally
have to bend double to make any progress. I spend a lot of time
on the cliffs, because my sheep are there. I graze the cliff from
Rhossili to the coastguard look-out, another fellow has the
stretch then to Fall Bay, and someone else the bit from Fall to
Mewslade. Then the three of us together use the Iley stream for
washing and dipping them. I remember we used to stand for
three or four hours in the water there, dashed cold it was too.
We'd be doing this for two or three days and then we'd clip
them, all by hand. Nowadays it's in and out quickly and off
with the wool. I've got a whole lot of that drystone walling to
keep an eye on. It's been there for centuries, and it's got a nasty
habit of collapsing here and there. Building these walls is a lost
art today, but I had to do so much of it, I got quite good. It is very
important you lay the stones in such a way that the wall will
lean out at the top, to stop the sheep running up and jumping in
over it. They are there to keep the sheep out you see. You have
to start by bringing the first three or four layers out, then you've
got a good chance.

If you spend any time down here you can see why there are no
trees anywhere near the sea. The winds. Except for the famous
ash tree, and that incidentally is, or was, in my farm yard. It was
often drawn and photographed, as the only tree to flourish at all
in these parts. And that because it was growing horizontally out of
a wall! I don't think it could ever have grown up straight, it
could never have reached any height on these cliffs. It must
have been a sapling that kept growing out of the wall sideways.
When I was a boy it was about thirty feet long, and I remember
it was a nuisance to the manoeuvering of a horse and cart in the
yard, the horse's mane would get tangled in the boughs, but it
was a challenge to us youngsters, he was considered a brave
chap who could walk along the full length of the trunk and
swing off the other end. It was much further off the ground in
those days. Well, sad to say, the old tree has gone now, a hole or
two opened up in the trunk and let in the rain, and gradually it's
been rotting away. In the end, a short time ago, someone took a

bulldozer into the yard, turned it round a bit awkwardly, and
that was the last of it. I don't expect we'll see a tree of that size
again in the village.

The strange thing about the wind here, though, is that when
it blows from the east or south-east, the sea under the cliffs is
like a lake, safe as anything for mooring. I mean, that's where
the limestone boats from Devon used to tie up for their loads, in
days gone by, that is. But no sooner does the wind shift round to
the west or south than the waves build up and it becomes a
proper trap for boats—they can't get round the Head. I remember one wreck we had there. I've been a member of the rocket
crew since I was sixteen, so I've seen a few wrecks on this bit of
coast. This was only a little boat, called the *Gloria*, she had
come in to shelter for a day and a half, for repairs. The wind
suddenly flew round and she couldn't get out for the breakers.
They called the rocket out, but we all stood on the top of the
cliff, helpless, the boat was much too close for us to fire a rocket
and too far away for throwing a lead. So they took to a small
boat, and four or five of them started to row ashore. Then they
lost their oars. Some of the rocket crew got down onto the beach
to run in and give them a hand. All they did in fact was to help
them in over the last few yards. But you should have seen the
Evening Post that night, telling the tale of how the brave Rhossili heroes had dashed into the boiling surf with the waves neck-
high to rescue the crew of the stricken ship! Without these great
fellows it seemed all the seamen would have been drowned.

Well, I think two or three of us might have just got our feet wet, but that's all. I've never believed anything I've read in the papers since then.

Not much excitement with the rocket crew these days. We get called out mostly now to look for lost kids and people falling over the cliffs, things like that.

*   *   *

My mother started taking visitors shortly after the First World War. She also kept a little shop and a tearoom, and provided hot water for picnics. Of course, the farm always came first, nothing was allowed to interfere with the farm jobs. They were always with us, after all. But in those days the bit of extra money was welcome, we couldn't have lived without it. Then, families used to come and stay for two or three weeks at least. They would find their own food and we would cook it and serve it for them. If they caught fish all the better. Salmon bass must have been more plentiful then, because I remember one fellow, he would come back with four lovely bass before I got out of bed in the morning!

The last war put an end to visitors for a bit. We got evacuees instead. We had four of them, the most of any house in the village. A family of two girls and another girl and a boy. They were Londoners, and they came from very poor families, but they were quite nice kids, really. They brought with them a few unpleasant things, like nits in the hair, impetigo, we all caught that, and measles, things we didn't have as children, we got then. We should have had three evacuees, but when they were brought to the door, there was this little girl on her own, no one wanted her . . . "Take her for a night," the fellow said, "till we can find somewhere". At first they wouldn't even undress and go to bed. They were not going to stay. "Oh no, tomorrow we're going back, we're not stopping here". But they settled in, and they were here for three years. The boy liked it so much here that he came back to work on the farm, for quite a time. He's in Australia now. We still hear from them all now.

After the war I was married, and then my wife carried on the family tradition. It became different then. People had cars, and the type of holiday changed. Though when we started they'd stay put for a fortnight and wouldn't even start up their cars until they left for home. Now it's quite different. We've got a few regulars, they are really in love with Gower, and the beaches. In the evenings they don't even go out for a drink, they stay chatting and playing cards till bedtime. No TV even. They are mostly the middle-aged ones. Very few children. Youngsters don't want to stay more than a day or two now. People generally just come for bed and breakfast and that, a day at a time. It's better for business in a way, because now the season begins in the middle of March and goes on until the middle of November. I must admit it would still be a poor living without taking visitors. The farm is only small, and we'd have had to develop it more commercially somehow, employ more labour, and that. You have to give up a lot if you take visitors, mind, a fair bit of sacrifice is needed, especially from my wife. We lose the best months of the year. But we quite like it, it's nice to meet people, we've been very lucky, I could reckon on one hand the people we shouldn't be keen on seeing again.

I don't suppose we appreciate Gower, that is its history and the legends and that, as much as our visitors do. We take it all for granted, like. But in our own way we feel more of a part of it. I love the hill and the cliffs, I know every inch of them. And that turf, so fine, and close and springy. It used to make me wild to see it, when people would come from all parts, dig it up and cart it away, for lawns and things. Little vans and lorries would come, men would cut out strips, roll them up and away to go. They've stopped all that now, thank heaven. When I am trailing up and down that turf on a tractor I make a point of never going twice in the same track. I watch it carefully, and if I do turn up a bit of it, I get off and push it back into place with my foot. No one else seems to bother though, they're slowly cutting it to pieces. I remember one boy I had, I said to him: "You take the plough along, I'll follow on". And on the way down he dropped the plough in the turf and turned up two furrows right along the cliff-top. I went mad. It took me an hour to turn them back. Luckily the turf was tough and it didn't break. Then I drove the tractor over it a few times. "What were you thinking of?" I asked him. "I just thought I'd clean the plough", he said. No feeling for it with the youngsters today.

RHONA RICHARDS

Land Girl

Born in Swansea 1922

I was living in Swansea when the war came, very much a townee, and I realised I'd be called up for something. So I applied for the WRENS and got accepted. But my mother's health wasn't too good, and she said: "Can't you think of something that will keep you near home?" So that's how I changed my mind. I had never had any experience of life in the open air nor any desire for it, I wasn't even interested in gardening. Some of my mother's people were farmers, I suppose it could have been the reason. Because I started thinking about the Land Army, when I was working in the office. And it so happened that a friend of mine had been evacuated to Rhossili, and when I went down to visit her one day she said she knew of a farmer who was looking for a land girl. "You'll be very comfortable at Jessamine Farm", she said. So that's how it came about. This farmer applied for me, and I was drafted into a farming life. The whole idea was to be near home, but as things turned out, I never lived at home again! I've never regretted it, mind, not one little bit.

Life on a farm shattered me at first, I must admit. I never realised it would be as hard as it turned out to be. And with the animals, I was frightened to death at the beginning, I don't mind telling you. For one thing, I found myself sitting under a cow, and never in my life had I been so near as that to a cow. I mean, looking at them in a field is one thing, and that used to scare me, but sitting right under one of the things with a bucket, that's very different! And then, trying to milk it is different again. In the end I really got to like the creatures, I always

talked to them, and I'm sure they used to like that, they respon-
ded to me and got to know my touch, no doubt about it. I did a
bit of everything on the farm, though I wasn't always very good,
I'd have a go, planting, hoeing, and picking potatoes and things.
But mainly I was the milk maid. I had to get the cows from the
field, feed them, milk them, take them back to the fields, clean
out the stalls. Then I used to deliver the milk around the village, all on foot, carrying it in big cans.

I'd never been to this village before, but I got to think it was
wonderful. Not so much the beaches, really, because I don't
swim. But I fell in love with the life here, and the inhabitants.
Especially with one of them. I used to see a young fellow passing by on a tractor. At first he'd just nod to me, then it came to
waving, then I'd see him at the whist drives they used to hold in
the village hall. Funnily enough we didn't meet at the dances,
we didn't dance, either of us. Anyway, that's how we got together, and we married in 1945. I had been a land girl for nearly
three years, then I became a farmer's wife. It didn't seem to
make a lot of difference, really, except that I spent the first years
of married life cutting sandwiches for the men going out to the
fields all day. Then in the evening they'd be back home, raven-
ously hungry again. I used to help too, planting and lifting potatoes, but they didn't make a slave of me.

I often think of what I'd have done if I'd had to leave farming
and go back to a town life. I don't think I could have stuck it for
a minute. It's been a strange thing, but I suppose fate gave me a
hankering for the outdoor life which I never knew I had.

VICTOR WATTERS

Experimental Farmer

Born at Pilton Green Smithy 1920

My grandfather was something of an individualist. He was a blacksmith by trade and he brought up his seven sons to have minds of their own. He even gave them unusual names: Lancelot, Cecil, Hubert, Messina, Abraham, Jasper and Bert, names which he got, so it is said, from serial stories in the church magazine. He'd walk three miles to church three times on a Sunday; he was Sunday School Superintendent for forty years, and he had read the Bible through once, and was half way through it for the second time. During the First World War all his sons registered as conscientious objectors. My father was arrested at the forge and because he wouldn't wear the King's uniform, he was taken to Wormwood Scrubs, where he had to do three months solitary confinement. Then he was moved to Scotland to work as smith on a cutting project. Eventually the Home Office put him with a farming family near Llanelli, where he stayed about twelve months, and this was his first real experience of farming outside his own home.

In 1921, home again, he took over Monksland Farm. And from then on he became interested in farming and ways of improving it. One of my first memories is of the Dutch tomato boxes that he collected, he'd bring them back from Swansea on Saturday after selling his eggs and butter and poultry in the town, and did I enjoy the fruit he used to buy with the takings! But these boxes he would use for chitting potatoes. I claim quite humbly that my father was the pioneer of chitting potatoes in Gower. In my bedroom, above the parlour, and my sister's, there were only two narrow paths between the boxes, one to the door and one to the window. They were piled up all around us. 'Catriola' and 'King Edward' were my father's favourites for competition work—he had soon become a great Gower Show man. 'Arran Pilot' was the rest of the crop. I remember Dick and Bess used to be the team he used to open up the rows.

My father was something of a pioneer in plant food ratios as well. No one knew what they really were at that time. He used to buy straight fertilizers in the form of two-cwt. sacks of sulphate of ammonia, superphosphate, and then there'd be guano, brought to us by the steam traction engine that later on would do the threshing for us. He'd tip all these fertilizers out onto the barn floor, and he'd mix them up with a shovel, trying out different proportions, working blindly, really. Then, through David Morgan's Farmers' Co-op at Reynoldston, one of several vain attempts to start up a Gower farmers' co-op, my father got in touch with an ICI fieldsman, Fuller Lewis by name, and he used to come to Monksland to talk to my father about fertilizers. I remember something of their conversations—that there's so much sulphate of ammonia equivalent to so much sunlight, phosphate is equivalent to food and rooting power, and potash is equal to so much vitamin, something like that. So the mixings on the barn floor became more scientific, and my father acquired a manure drill the like of which I never saw before or since. The container moved, the rest of the machine was stationary, but as the wheel went along, drawn by a horse, the container lifted and there was a series of spikes about three inches long, which revolved and flicked the manure over the back of the machine as it went along. This was used at different settings to make different quantities according to the sowing. After that we had a so-called Demonstration Field at Monksland, and in 1928 there was a big demonstration held, for all the farmers in the area to come to our farm and see the areas where the different sowings and different applications of fertilizer could be inspected and compared. Then they were all entertained to tea by my mother. It was a big day, and there was a photograph of the gathering in the local paper. It was a unique event in the farming life of Gower.

In the spring of 1933, I was still in school. I had just had the result of the 11 plus exam, and I had failed. Ever practical, my father came home from Swansea one Saturday and told me: "I've bought a farm for you". It so happened that Miss Evans the headmistress had given me a paper asking my father if he would let me try an exam for Pontardawe School—this was open to border-line cases—but he distinctly refused: "No, you've failed one exam, you won't have the chance of another one. I've bought this farm for you to work on". It was called Lake Farm, of 45 acres, and not very far from the school. So for the twelve months or so before I had left school, I used to look after a large number of sows and a boar that had been moved down to Lake. I'd call there on my way to school in the morning, on my bike, to feed these pigs, back there at lunch-time, and again after school in the evening.

I left school, and my father was getting more and more active in the N.F.U. He was also very interested in the education of those farmers who showed they were keen to learn. There were numerous lectures organized, through the Director of Education, on all aspects: fruit tree growing, horticulture, poultry husbandry and dressing, butter-making, and clean milk production, and each lecturer in turn would spend some time with us at home. Professor Stapleton, from Aberystwyth and Professor Ashby used to come to Monksland to meet my father and he did a lot of work with them on the introduction of different strains of grasses.

My father was very keen on the competition that the Gower Show used to offer. I believe it was a sort of challenge for him, because he'd been brought up as a blacksmith, then came the war years, and after all that he had become a farmer. He had brought a fresh approach to it, and was anxious to prove he could succeed. Besides this, of course, he was a great man for detail, and thoroughness. I've got the tickets from the earliest Gower Shows, and in one particular year he won seventeen Firsts, one Second and one Third. The prizes in the early days used to be something like 5 cwts. of fertilizer, 1 cwt. of soap, three silver teapots, two sets of carvers, biscuit barrels, I've got them all about the house here . . . His favourite mangel would be Garden's Lemon Globe, the swede would be Magnificent, and the field entry for potato King Edward. Then Majestic, a kidney, superseded Gladstone, which was susceptible to blight, because of its size and cooking qualities. Wheat would be White Victor, very good for milling, and my mother would bake bread from the White Victor, grinding it in the old Bam-

Hubert Watters at Gower Show, early 1930s.

ford Number Two mill driven by a Lister 5 h.p. engine, then sieving it, and baking cake from the coarser flour and bread from the finer. Barley was Plumage Archer, this was good barley for competition work. Some local farmers followed father's work closely, but his fellow competitors at the Show were only the usual few. I think Sid Thomas was the first one to realise that a spud should be planted upright on its end! And a few came regularly back and fore to Monksland to see: ''How's thine as compared with mine, boy?'' Those who competed were tremendously keen, but there was always good sportsmanship. No enmity at all. I remember I used to get teased on the way to school before the Show: ''Dang thee, boy, thee's put that old barley in water again'', implying that last year's had been soaked in water in readiness. Impossible, of course, but that's the sort of leg-pulling that went on. There were some keen mangel-growers about, too, but my father was always regarded as the mangel-king of Gower.

At the same time he was very politically-minded. The

old *Glasgow Forward* with its serrated edge, and the *New Leader* with its bold title letters were two papers that came regularly to our house. Conversation at home would be often political, every news would be listened to and the political administration would always be under fire, and the effects on the family would be discussed. Not on the farmworker, but upon us as a farming family at home, as a community. This awareness of the effects of decisions made elsewhere, this interpretation of political moves, of cause and effect, certainly made us more conscious of what was going on around us.

But it did him no good at all with the Penrice Estate. As a result of Court Leet administration there was a prejudice, and enmity if you like, between Pritchard the agent and the boys of our family, who were all wanting farms. I believe it was politically instigated. My father happened to be Poor Law Officer for Rhossili and Porteynon, and he was well aware of the appalling state of some of the estate's dwelling-houses. It could have been one of several things that brought him into conflict with Pritchard.

All this has coloured my approach to farming, I must say. My father's interest in ideas, his need to experiment, the visitors to his farm, all of it has left its mark on me. And I hope I've been able to pass something of these attitudes on to my children. I believe I have. My son, for example, is beginning to show some talent in stock-judging. In this year's Royal Welsh Show he and his Young Farmers' Club brought back that silver bowl, the highest award in the stock-judging competition.

In 1936, when I was sixteen I was a founder member of the first Young Farmers' Club in Gower. Bridgend was the first one in Glamorgan, we were the second. We had thirty-five members to start, I remember my receipt number was 5. I got a lot of benefit from our meetings, in particular the practice in stock-judging. And a knowledge of grass breeds. When we went round different farms the course leader would grab hold of a bunch of grass and give a handful to each of us. "Now how many of these can you identify?", would be his first question and this created an interest, certainly in me, not only for the livestock, but for the quality of the grass they ate, and in fact for everything around us. The main aim of stock-judging was to give one the practical ability to view an animal and appreciate it from its shape, its quality and its trueness to type. We had first of all to view four animals of any breed, for a minute, then stand the four side by side, labelled A, B, X and Y. You were given two minutes to handle the animals, then a further minute to check your decisions. You'd then be given a card, and on this you'd place them in your order. You'd hand in your card, and each of you had to give a verbal account of your placing. The competition between members was keen, so it sharpened your wits. I found this good. There was no jealousy or malice, as there is often now, it was all done in good spirit and humour. Another thing it did for me—I had a stammer in those days, but having to give this verbal assessment before the group gave me more confidence, and my stammer disappeared gradually.

No doubt of it, the Y.F.C. gave a tremendous lift to the education of the agricultural community, just at a time when it was sorely needed. Up till then it was commonly said: "There's a farmer's son, you can see by the way he walks, his hands in his pockets, his shoulders hunched and watching his toes coming forward".

Where are we going, I often ask myself, with pesticides and weed-killers? It worries me. Our pressure once was to find the men to do the cleaning and the hoeing, and to cover the cost. Then came the weedkillers and it was found that they could do away with inter-crop cultivation at one stroke. But at the same time as we've been getting rid of our annual weeds, we have created a perennial weed problem which we're not going to get rid of so easily. Instead of the groundsel, we've now got black grass, couch grass, deep-rooted grasses. We started with a weed-killer that would cover seven annual weeds, but soon we got a spectrum weedkiller that would deal with seventeen, and many areas are now bedevilled with grass weeds, a much greater problem. Stronger weedkillers mean more expense. We've gone away, too, from the rotation of crops, three-year, five year, all have been discarded, and it's repeat, repeat, repeat the crop for up to seven years, and as a result the weed problem has been building up, because there's been no *cleaning* year,

Glamorgan Social Sciences Students, 1932.

and in spite of all the scientific 'improvements', the control of weeds is taking more and more time and energy.

Gradually it is being appreciated that we have to go back to clover, to introduce nitrogen into the soil. But now they have to inoculate the clovers against the diseases that have been introduced for attacking the various types of clover. Incidentally, I was interested to see that oil seed, rape, has been introduced. I recently tasted honey from it, and though the honey was beautifully white, I must say I found the taste somewhat oily!

When I come to think of the future of farming, I can't help asking: "Where are we going?" I sometimes think that the replacement of the horse by the tractor was the turning point. We had a debate in the club once on "The horse or the tractor?" and one fellow said: "If there wasn't a seat on the back of the damn thing, they wouldn't sell so many of them". You see, we used to breed a horse, breed a colt, and we'd sell the colt. Maybe two in the year. Still, we always had a youngster to break in, and we had to see to it that there *was* a youngster to break in. And so maintain a continuity of horse power. The tractor came. We bought our first Fordson in 1940 for £150. We used it for ten years. We put tyres on it for another £100 and we sold it for twice what we gave for it. Then you could sell a horse or two to buy a tractor, today you've got to sell half your farm. The balance of values is quite topsy-turvy. And it concerns me deeply. When I look at what I've got . . . I mean, a farmer only dies worth money. While he's here he's got nothing in his hands. It's only figures we handle, and directly this year's figures become less than last year's, I'm standing still, going backwards in fact. It's a strange world.

There are no teachers in the family, but education is in my blood, I suppose, and I feel very keenly about it. Short of being a teacher myself, I've done the next best thing, I've recently been instrumental in opening a Farm Trail, for children, and for visitors, beginning and ending at my farm. There are at the moment only fourteen Farm Trails in Britain, and ours is the first in Glamorgan. I am a producer of food; you, say, are a consumer. Unless we are allowed to understand one another's problems, we're not going to get anywhere unless we encourage a better appreciation of each other's lives. The idea of the Farm Trail came out of my activities on the Farm Tourism Panel for Wales. The Countryside Commission got in touch with the N.F.U. headquarters, and I was asked if I would help form such a Trail in Gower. It was a question not only of having a farm large enough to contain it, but also of getting co-operation enough to supervise it. I was lucky in both of these, so a Farm Trail has now been opened along an existing bridle way and footpath, and offers the walker a view of eight farms as he makes his way over the path for six and a half miles. There are eighteen stiles—we were only able to retain one stone stile—marking the way, and there are, on your left as you go, posts every hundred yards with the top 18 inches painted white. There is a brochure available pointing out what to look out for in the way of crops, or soil, or flowers, or birds and animals, and you can see pretty well all you are likely to meet at other sites. The flora and fauna are not very different from other similar routes. I am delighted that the response has been tremendous already. One good thing is, when a bunch of school children turn up at the farm asking if they can look around, the Trail is a means of making sure they can't mistake the recognised path; and it teaches them to use their eyes to look for natural landmarks instead of following street lamps. All kinds of people, of all ages, have used the Trail, and several schools have adopted it as a special project for their out-of-door activities.

I have, of course, by organising all this laid myself open to criticism from my own fraternity: one fellow, not of this parish, but an old N.F.U. member told me off quite severely for "opening up footpaths to the public". I must say though that, in the main, I have had the utmost co-operation from the farmers over whose land it goes. Let's hope the exercise will educate, not only the visitors, but the farmers themselves!

You see, I reckon that we farmers have been apt to shut our gates to outsiders for too long, and forgotten that there's no longer any secret about what happens on this farm or that, what with our returns to the Ministry, and to research bodies, they know all the facts and figures. I suppose traditionally the greatest enemy a farmer had was his next door neighbour: especially in a closed community like Gower. But I'm proud of my job, and I want to show people how it's run. The more professionalism I can show to the consumer public, the greater respect they will feel for the farmer. "Oh, you farmers are rolling in it" is a common chide, and they don't realise how little return we are getting for the amount we have invested.

As a farmer I have to wear two uniforms: one inside my farm gates, when I am dealing with Nature, because I find Nature very honest, but as soon as I go outside the gate I have to put on another uniform, a sort of armour, a defence against my fellow men.

Note
Mr Watters' son, Clive, is continuing the policy of spreading information about the agricultural community to visitors who are interested to learn. He has now set up, at Lake Farm, Llanddewi, a 'Gower Museum', where old implements and photographs are on display.

CHRISTOPHER BEYNON
Young farmer
Born in Rhossili (Great Pitton Farm) 1937

There have been Beynons at this farm since the eighteenth century, and the farm itself goes back another two hundred years again. So when I took over, in my teens, really, there was a very strong family tradition here, and that was—to farm well. My father died suddenly when I was away at school. Only twelve I was, and my grandfather was about to retire. He had achieved the position of being one of the better, and bigger, farmers in Gower, and he was very proud of this. I don't think money came into it primarily, but in the end they made enough to live a little better perhaps than some of the smaller farmers. When father took over in 1933 or so, he became one of the first to grow vegetables in Gower. The war came, and more and more vegetables had to be produced, so grandfather took a back

Great Pitton Farm, pre-1930.

seat. He was a stock man himself, he never really came to terms
with the change; I don't think he ever saw the farm as an arable
farm. He never learned to drive a tractor, there was very little
ploughing anyway before the 30s. Even until he died he used to
go out in his horse and cart, he and his brother, every day, whatever the conditions, to inspect the animals in the fields. Back
about 10 o'clock. He even used to have his own roads made for
the horse and cart. We've ploughed up a lot of them now. I spent
hours as a youngster breaking stones for these special tracks of
his. He used to pride himself that immediately he looked at a
field of sheep or cattle he could tell if there was anything wrong
with one of the animals. He loved animals.

When my father died, as I say, I was away at school, and I had
no idea of the significance of it at all. One holiday he was there,
working normally, the next holiday he wasn't. It didn't dawn
on me for some time what a difference this would make at
home. Mother was a farmer's daughter and she wanted to carry
on for my sake, but she was becoming terribly anxious about it.
I came away from school, at 14, without any training as it were;
my grandfather had retired, and for the next six years or so I

lived an exceedingly anxious existence. The war years, when you could sell anything, were past. Costs were going up. And I became the boss—at 14! Of course I never had thought of doing anything else eventually. I suppose I was never allowed to have any doubts about what was expected of me. And now, in my first twelve months of farming, all my mother could drill in me was, whatever you do, you've got to do it well! Time after time. But I couldn't have had better advice really.

Those first years were absolute chaos. One crisis after the other. We were struggling so hard, but we were out of date with mechanisation, a lot of it had to be replaced or renewed, we'd got so behind . . . I know I drove myself off my feet almost, for years. Complete lack of experience, and over-enthusiasm, those were my faults. Wanting to do things too fast, and the wrong way, just having no idea of the problems I was up against. For a long time, too, I had a lot of difficulty finding my position with the men. A number of them had been here for a long time. I had to gain their respect, and find my position either in front of them, or alongside them, or behind them. This took many years, and many heart-breaks, because they could shoot you down so easily. I won my way eventually, I think by hard work and application. By doing it well, whether it was picking pot-atoes or dealing with a calf. And ever since it has been my aim . . . every crop in at the right moment, treating the ground per-fectly, careful preparation; it's the only way to efficiency and profit.

I married at 22. Fortunately to a girl who though she knew nothing about farming had an enquiring mind. We increased our land by buying a 110 acre-farm adjoining it. We started taking professional advice now and began to specialise. To drop all the crops that father and grandfather had grown—parsnips, cabbage, carrots, onions as well as the ducks and hens and turkeys, all complicated, high-labour crops, and to plan the extra acreage. In war-time they grew sugar beet, and maize as well! But they've all gone from the farm now. Ever since, we've specialised in beef cattle and lamb production. We grow more corn now and the stock numbers have gone up four-fold in the last few years. One difficulty now is where to stop in the stocking density, we can keep so many animals! At least we can grow plenty of grass in these parts, but now the hedges are falling down, we have to put so many animals in a field to eat the grass. This is a growing problem with us now.

We buy in bull calves at a week old, rear them on artificial milk, give them specially prepared cake for a few weeks, and our own corn and hay on their first winter inside. They spend one summer out on grass, and the second winter they're fattened off into beef with barley and silage. It's a totally planned system, we don't rely on uncertain factors, like when is the cow going to calve, or is it going to be a cow or a bull calf? I like everything planned. We had calves in last week, and I can tell almost to the week when those calves are going to turn into money. I've set up a new silage plant at another farm we bought, three miles away. With a modern silo you can turn good grass into silage without fail. But in horse and cart days you couldn't handle loads of wet heavy grass, it was completely impossible. And even in the early 50s it was difficult, when 40 h.p. was enormous power for a tractor. But now we have tractors of 80 h.p. And with more land you can justify more and

Early Fordson tractor with binder in use on Great Pitton Farm.

larger machinery, a combine harvester for example. Did we buy the extra units for that reason? I sometimes wonder. It's really all happened in fact quite naturally. We were young, borrowed a lot of money; they were big steps to take. But I've reached the age already when I'm not so keen on the hard work, but I enjoy management. I've never given it much thought, but I always have been ambitious in this way. In these parts this is an unusual way of farming, land doesn't change hands all that frequently. It could be that working with older people helped to give me my head, my ideas were completely fresh and unprejudiced. So I had no hesitation when the opportunity came.

My grandfather would be pleased to know we'd turned back to stock. But would he have accepted our type of farming? I think in time he would have seen the value of it. But our farming now is a job where nobody ever need touch a thing. We can get all our winter feed in and stored without anyone lifting an ounce of it. The men have got a comfortable seat on the tractor, and they have to do nothing else. No pitching, no forking, no handling of food-stuffs. All changed.

*   *   *

One constant, of course, is the geography of this part of Gower. We're frost-free, so early potatoes are very much a proposition. At my farm three miles inland, for instance, you couldn't dream of getting earlies within six weeks of when we get them out here. The year I bought that farm there was a disastrous frost on May 24th. Here we didn't have a trace. Potatoes are now, our major crop, but they're an expensive one in effort and cash. A strange thing to say, but we are on potatoes twelve months of the year. I've bought seed now for my ware crop in two years' time. We're chitting seed now, on every wet day. We look after them carefully through the winter, a fair bit of work this. But they really are our most precious commodity. We can lift early potatoes now within a day or two of Pembrokeshire. And we haven't got their transport difficulties.

In fact, one big thing that affects your thinking is that anything you produce in Gower is virtually saleable on your doorstep. Having all those customers within 30 miles of you is a terrific backing.

Being on the edge of the sea, too, has its mixed blessings. We get a lot of humid weather, which is difficult to live with, as a farmer. This is why I now prefer silage to the traditional hay making. When a friend of mine in the Vale of Glamorgan would be baling, the grass here would be too damp to cut, though the sun would be shining. We have to choose varieties of corn— low-yielding varieties even—that will put up with the humidity. It affects your judgement in many ways. Then we get the wind—that's our biggest enemy of all. A salt gale can wipe out a crop, blackens everything, often in high summer . . .

Labour is not really a problem with us . . . the fact that we are biggish, and mechanised, so most of the work can be done by someone sitting on a tractor, that attracts labour. People don't like hard work these days, so the small farmer who has to hump every bag of fertilizer off a lorry can't offer much. We'd be in trouble ourselves if we didn't have a few tied cottages. I know they've come under fire, but we've had no problems, ever. With a reasonable employer and a fair employee it works quite satisfactorily, I think. For casual labour, for potato-picking, that seems to be a woman's job in these parts. We get cockle-pickers from North Gower on the job, fantastic backs they've got, made of rubber, backache never seems to worry them! We've had the same family coming over for nearly twenty years.

I must admit I'm a bit of an isolationist as far as the farming world at large is concerned. We're a big family now, and a young one, and with the work on the farms, it's not easy. And I'm not madly interested in politics of any kind. In Farmers Union and Young Farmers meetings I think people talk too much, they make far too much noise about too little. I mind my own business and work as hard as I can within my own scope. It gives me the greatest pleasure to see a job done soundly, and the most anguish to see one done badly. Maybe I can show an example to some one in this way? I am concerned in adapting my farm to the economic position of the moment, rather than in belly-aching about not having the conditions we would like to see. It's very selfish, I know, but when I once did take up office with the N.F.U. I got so frustrated, I retired and went back to concentrate on the real job. Not that I am unwilling to help others. I make school-children welcome, and students. I always employ a pre-college student every year, because they have difficulty in finding a farm to work on, I enjoy this, and I feel it is one of the few altruistic or philanthropic things I can do to help the industry. I give these everything I've got, they come in as callow schoolboys, just out of A level, and at the end of the year they go out as young men. A fantastic transformation. They learn a tremendous amount about a completely new way of life, more than in any subsequent year, so one who came back told me. It's good for them, it's good for me, and it's good for the men. It's not only the techniques and the knowledge, it's the contact with responsibility, and commercial pressures. They still go away knowing very little anyway, but they're on the right road. We could replace a student with a man, but it's one of the things I feel I can do, and I shall carry on doing it.

My life is in a way lonelier than my grandfather's. He used to like going to mart, meeting other farmers. It used to be a social occasion, and many of them used to do some business on the side. But much of that is gone now. Anyway I see markets as inefficient time-wasters, and even if I enjoyed them I wouldn't allow myself the luxury. If I'm selling an animal for meat, to take it to mart only adds expense to the process, and that goes through to the customer. To convey the animal, waste a day there, then have it taken away for slaughter, with an auctioneer's fees on the top of it all, it's a totally unnecessary performance. The phone is my market. A few minutes on that and I can make more radical decisions than I would standing around waiting for things to happen. I like going to the local Farmers' Club, and I learn a lot that way, but to some extent I find the attitude of many of the younger farmers puzzling. They lack knowledge, their output falls short, so does the general appearance of their farms, and the weed and the filth they allow to pass, and yet they don't seem to want to know what's wrong. Can't they see that it's not happening everywhere? They don't even look for advice.

Most of my technical knowledge has come from the Ministry's Advisory Service, especially at the beginning. I really owe them a tremendous lot. I've certainly had more than my fair share of their time, but in return I have done a lot of work for them, trying out grass seeds, sprays, fertilizers and that. I came in, you see, with a blank slate, I was hungry for knowledge. Pride didn't matter. A lot of farmers feel there's something wrong in asking the Advisory Office in. I feel sorry for these Advisory chaps, they can see trouble, they know there's trouble, and they could help so much, but they're not called in, nothing they can do about it. But I left school eager to learn— and do well. I still am a glutton for knowledge. I could never accept, you see, that things can go wrong, I simply don't accept it. If the baler starts dropping bales without the string on, I just refuse to believe that it can happen. I keep piling this into the men. It gets on everybody's nerves, I know, but that's me. I've got to stop to get it put right. Same with a crop. If it grows nine-tenths of the time, and then suddenly stops, why? I just have to find out. In the early days I was lucky—the farm was strong enough to weather my mistakes. It had inborn stability, and enough character to carry me; we had good men, too. No getting away from it, we lived on the fertility of this farm for several years. We did the most abominable bits of husbandry, but we got away with it. Even now, if we dash in a crop in a hurry on this farm, we can get away with it. But on any of the other farms, we wouldn't. They just haven't got the stamina to face adverse conditions.

There was one bit of technique we discovered on our own, though. In the handling of early potatoes. We discovered by chance something we've since had confirmed as a fact: that the potato has a physiological age. Years ago when we were in the cauliflower trade, we'd grow cauliflower till the end of April or so, and that would be the last crop of the previous year's sowing. Then we used to put in our seed potatoes. It wasn't too late, and seed potatoes would be just big enough in the autumn to be lifted. Anyway, we gave up cauliflower, so we decided to put in the seed, well over a month earlier than before. And what a splendid crop we got! For the next season. We went on, then put them in earlier, burned off the haulms earlier, put them into trays a bit earlier, and blow me, before we knew it we were growing early potatoes. We had altered the physiological age, so they told us, and improved the strain.

One thing worries us tremendously now. Why are the hedges dying, and the bushes? It's a tree-less area, anyway, but I know we are killing off wild plants in the hedges and it makes me very sad. First, as I said, it's the sheer weight of animals we graze in a field, and the other thing is, of course, that we have to use sprays. No one goes out now with a spade to build up the banks, we just can't afford the labour. As it is we've got miles and miles of drystone walls to maintain, and we look after them. Many don't bother. We don't want to kill off a single thing on the farm, anything. But it is an awful problem.

*   *   *

As you can imagine, I can't relax a moment on the farm. Come to that, neither could my father or my grandfather. I can go out sometimes and I can feel myself spoiling a most beautiful day, because everywhere I look I see trouble. It's an awful habit. You go into a herd of cattle, and you spot the two poor ones at the back, you walk into a field of sheep, you see the lame ones. You don't see the hundreds looking so well. Very occasionally I do say: "What a marvellous place to farm". It's always there, I suppose, in the back of my mind, but I'm always striving for perfection, too much, perhaps. It's not a money thing. I just hate to see anything done badly. It's for this reason I've taken up rally-driving in the last few years. Funny way to relax you may say, but it has worked. It has cost me a lot of money and it is a bit of a drain, but it has brought out a lot of good in me, and oddly enough, in the men. Because I used to do, still do, too much thinking for them, though I try not to. So when I had a rally on, I went, whether it was harvest or not. It made me real-ise that things would carry on without me, and in this way re-laxed my attitudes. I'm nothing like as tense as I was when I was 25. Then I never went anywhere. And I've had the satis-faction of doing well at rallying, got away with several trophies and things, and had a lot of fun against the best amateurs in the country.

My wife is Welsh . . . but I haven't the least feeling about
being Welsh. If I'm in Cardigan or Builth I feel as if I'm in a foreign country, out of things. She loves it. She helps me a lot—to
ask why. If she thinks there is a weak spot this year, say the
lambs, or disease in the cereals, we have to examine the problem over the past year, in depth, and see what efforts we can put
into rectifying it. One of her things, too, and she's absolutely
right, is to ask, if you have your own secret techniques, why tell
anyone else about it? Not long ago I discovered how to grow my
early potatoes earlier than anyone else, and the first thing I have
to do is give a talk to other farmers about it. She thought I was
mad. My only defence was that nine out of ten never take your
advice and follow it through, so it didn't matter. Perhaps I am
becoming a bit more cagey. Anyway, after a number of trials I
still go for some really old varieties, like Home Guard and Red
Royal. From the forties. That's one secret . . . Another thing she
feels strongly about is Sunday working. When it started she
thought it was terrible, but I didn't. You see our family has
lived with the fact that John Wesley once preached in our
kitchen—we still have the pulpit chair he used—so before our
time, grandfather, and my father, kept the Sabbath religiously.
They would never think of going out on a Sunday to work. I
remember the arguments I used to have with my mother about
getting hay in on a Sunday: "It is hay, it is going to rain, so
surely it's the right sensible thing to do". But there's been a
gentle drift, and once the first crack came, any job that really
needed doing has been done on a Sunday. Now, my wife com-
plains, they're even coming to collect animals on Sunday.
Mind you, it's not entirely out of religious feeling, she just believes we should have a rest day in the pattern of the week. I
hated going to chapel as a boy, so I've rarely been since. Though
in my own way, on the farm, working with Nature, I do have
my private leanings to religion. But I don't know how to fulfil
them. I've just kept my Christianity to my dealings with
people.

We have been blessed with four daughters, but no sons. So
what about the future? Well, we're leaving it very much open,
and neither encouraging nor discouraging them, to make it

their future. We don't really expect it to come off. But they
spend a lot of time with me outside, when they are home. They
are away at school, so I spend a lot of effort in making them feel
they belong here. With the older ones I can talk to them in
depth about farming, and the eldest has an excellent grasp of
what is going on and why. As good as any boy of her age would
be. I write to them all every week without fail, and it's all about
farming and its problems. That's my gossip anyway, I can't
share anything else with them. A woman could easily run this
farm now, better than I can in a way, so . . . we shall have to wait
and see.

PART IV

Community Life

JACK BEVAN

Plumber

Born in Rhossili 1900

My grandfather built the house we lived in, and it was held on a three lives lease, himself, my grandmother and my father. But we had bad luck in that. Because my father died when he was 42, so that meant the house would have to go back to the Estate. If my father had lived as long as my mother, there'd have been a hundred years lease, but what happened now was that they wanted to charge an extra rent, of £2.10s. But mother went to see Miss Talbot, and she let us have it for 30/- a year. I mean, we had built it ourselves after all. That was in 1904, about the hardest time there was for any farmer—but we survived. My mother had been left with six children—and they're all alive today incidentally, all about eighty and all living within yards of each other here—but that was the struggle of my young life. A farm of thirty acres, and no man, so I don't remember ever not having to work hard. Up before seven every morning, feed the 'things' before going to school, clean them out, and let them out to the stream that came down past our door. I remember I was a martyr to chilblains in those days and oh, the agony of trying to get my feet into the heavy boots that had been drying on the pentan (hob). And I used to hold the end of the leather lace in the candle flame to make it stiff enough to find the eyelet holes.

The stream, which came from a spring at 'Windy Walls', was called the 'Shute'* and my mother was known as 'Jane the Shute' because that's where we lived. Later on, the Estate put down a pipe and a village tap, and the tap was on the pine end of our house. This was a godsend to us, and the village. There wasn't a pool in the village, you see, because of the contours of the ground. You notice how the village is grouped around the lower slopes of the hill, and that is where in fact the original springs of water came out of the hill. Water has always gov-

*Pronounced 'Shut'.

Middleton, Rhossili, *ca.* 1900 : view down lane towards the 'shute'.

erned the life of the village. The villagers would go up and clean the streams that overflowed from the wells. Rhossili had one fairly good well up on the hill, that's how they fed their stock. Then further along, near the Old Rectory, is the Iley stream. That was considered to be the best water of all, it was always very cold. Before he died, my father was in hospital in Swansea, and mother would go and see him every Saturday, and she had to take a little can of Iley water for him, because he believed it was so much better than any other. The other Rhossili water wasn't considered so good. The coldest water of all was at Talgarth's Well. We used to fetch water from there in hot weather to cool the butter churn. Oh yes, water was the life of the village. We take so much for granted now.

How the stock managed is a great wonder to me now. I mean, if you've got cattle today they're drinking even in the middle of the night. You can wake up and hear the water running through the mains in the stillness of the night. Whereas we fattened two cattle each winter, and fed them on sliced or pulped swedes and chaff, and never gave them any water, right through the winter. I'm thinking, if we'd had given them a bucket of water twice a day they'd have fattened twice as quick. They used to be moaning, moaning, they were obviously thirsty, but we thought of course that the moisture from the swedes was enough. I'm afraid our fat cattle were never very fat, because we couldn't afford to buy any special feed for them. They'd be sold in February then, the butcher would come down from Swansea and strike a bargain, we used to get roughly £11.10s. or £12 for a bullock. You'd let them out then on the day before the Saturday you had to deliver them, twelve o'clock at Parkmill. They'd have a bit of a run and they'd go round and round the yard, it was like a rodeo, over the dung hills and up and down, galloping wild, and breathless. Then off we'd go the next morning, and for the first mile you could hardly keep up with them but by the time you got to Parkmill they'd be walking like cripples. It was one of my most gruelling jobs of the year. Outside the pub they'd have a rest for an hour or so, then the drovers would take them and pay you, in golden sovereigns neatly wrapped up by the bank, with a little seal, and you'd be ready to set out on the

Middleton, Rhossili, *ca.* 1920 : Lower Shop in the foreground, with Vanguard bus at The Bank in the background.

Gower Inn, Parkmill, *ca.* 1910

eleven miles home again. And your twenty-two sovereigns would be so heavy in your little pocket, by the time I reached home in my short trousers the money used to be rubbing my groin so badly I had to hold on to it to stop it chafing the skin. I once had a big blister this way. There were one or two for company, but those with fatter cattle wouldn't want to come with us, because the thinner cattle could half kill the fatter ones before we got half way; they'd want to go more slowly.

A job I used to dislike more than anything was grinding corn with our very primitive contraption . . . it was a rotating pole outside the barn, that was pulled round by a horse on a track, with a diameter of about twenty feet. And he'd walk round, turning the spindle. But the old horse would only go round if a boy was there to touch him up with a stick. Oh that was a tedious job, the bane of my life it was. If we wanted to grind wheat into flour we'd take it to the Middle Mill at Burry Green. 'Lizzie the Mill' was very good to us. Auntie Lizzie we used to call her, we didn't pay her for grinding, she would just take a portion of our sack for her pigs and poultry.

Some harvests would be very poor, you may have cut your wheat first week in August and if it came to rain you couldn't get it in for three weeks or a month, and by that time it had started to grow out or even go black, then you knew you were in for a terrible winter for bread. The loaf would be soggy and it would have a black seam right round it from top to bottom. That would be your bread for the rest of the winter. But we were fortunate in that Auntie Lizzie would often 'make a mistake', and mix a bucketful of our wheat with a bucketful of somebody else's, and keep the worst for her pigs, and it was about fit for them.

I remember a bakery opening at Reynoldston before the First World War and they used to deliver bread round the villages, one day a week in a trap, and oh, it was so good to buy a loaf of white bread, threepence or fourpence it was. Wonderful. My grandfather used to get a loaf every week till he died, and we'd call in to see grandma so that she could give us a slice of white bread, oh boy, was it a treat? Before the First World War even the better off people only ate white bread on Sundays. And even when it became more widely used the bran was left in, which made it very coarse. Barley was used to make a flat bakestone loaf about one inch thick. There was a brick oven for baking in every farmhouse. They'd put down a floor of fire-bricks, then make a heap of sand as a kind of mould, and then build the bricks over in an arch about 18ins. high, and big enough inside to bake nine or ten loaves. The oven was heated up with sticks from the beach or burnt furze stumps ''smitty sticks'', these would be burned inside until the bricks were almost white hot, then the embers would be scraped out and the loaves put in. The door was sealed with clay and that would be left then for two hours. When the bread was ready it'd be taken out and the sticks that were to be used next time were put in to be well baked in readiness for the next bread-making.

The big changes in farming came here in the nineteen twenties, of course, with motor haulage. Before that things hadn't changed for centuries, I should think; since early eighteen hundreds. As things were, the only things that were saleable up to then were wheat, barley (for brewing), beef, mutton, with a few

eggs, poultry and a bacon pig or so. There were 3,000 sheep in
the parish in my young days, usually small Welsh Mountain,
and they'd all be out on the hill or the cliffs, except when they
were lambing. Then a few farmers kept ponies running wild on
the commons, they'd be rounded up once a year, and as three-
year-olds they'd be sold at the Reynoldston Harvest Fair. Two
interesting features in the farming up to the end of the century
had been the type of ploughing known as 'eight furrow ridging',
and the use of guano as fertilizer. The first was practised by
some on wet land. Four furrows would be ploughed around a
'back'. The backs would be about eleven feet apart, leaving a
'hinten' or a channel where the outer furrows were parted.
Many old grass fields still show this narrow ridging and many
think it was a form of drainage. But an old farmer assured me
that the reason for it was, that, when they sowed their wheat in
the autumn in wet weather, they could stand in the hinten and
cover the corn by hacking the furrows with a hoe, as the ground
would be too wet for the horses to harrow it.

For fertilizing then there was the farmyard humus, lime from
the lime kilns, and this guano stuff. This was very strong and
very popular, but you had to buy it. It came from a Pacific
island. I don't know how it was discovered that it made field
manure, but a flourishing trade in it grew up, and Captain
Tucker Griffiths used to bring it back as ballast, to Swansea. It
was quite remunerative, he told me. They used to get in close to
this island, down there somewhere, and load it into bags.
Trouble was that the men used to be overcome by the fumes it
let off, sulphur, and it used to make their noses bleed. They
couldn't do a thing without masking their faces with linen.
Wonderful thing to bring as ballast though, it cost them nothing, you see. And tremendous as a fertilizer. If you sowed it in
the potato rows one year, you could see it in clear little ridges in
the rising corn the following year. If you could afford to buy it,
of course. Greening would bring a load of it to Pitton Cross on
top of the hill, with his traction engine. He'd blow his whistle
and the farmers would come for it with their horses, as the contraption couldn't come down into the village, the road was only
a narrow lane then. But farmers were so poor they couldn't

afford to buy enough of it. It was the old vicious circle. If they could have afforded more manure, they'd have got better crops, more hay and corn, more stock, and then more money to buy more manure the next year. Mind you, I think they were a bit short-sighted in that. They should have bought more, it was a good investment.

Almost every farm worker had a pigsty, and a good bit of garden. He'd have a row of potatoes in the farmer's field and he'd grow a couple of mangels in any place he could, to feed his pig through the winter. He could let the pig roam in the summer time, on the hill or the common. Bring him in at night. But feeding was a constant problem. If you can get a pig now about February, then feed him with all you can find in the way of scraps, even the washing-up water from the dishes—we never used soap for washing-up, that was water for the pig, save that, because there'd be a few scraps or a bit of bread or a bit of cabbage in it, and he'd get all the small potatoes, things like that. Some women used to go down to the sands and collect limpets, bags and bags of them, the pig would get those. He'd go through

Pigs at Murton.

the summer all right, feeding outside, on grass and roots, then you'd bring him in in September. By that time you'd have gleaned some barley and things, until he'd come now to the cold weather, and come big enough. Then back of November you'd kill him, then salt him down, and the circle would begin all over again. And you'd have your boiled bacon, a few eggs from your chickens, and perhaps a drop of milk from the farm, though a lot of people drank their tea without milk in those days. It was only 1d a pint, but many never bothered. But thanks to the pig, they kept body and soul together. Then again, a farm worker would get a bit of wool by plucking a dead sheep on the hill or cliffs, he had a right to do this. After a day, you can get more wool, and cleaner, from a dead sheep than if you sheared a live one. And any wool he'd find on the hedges or the furze, he'd collect that, and wash it, then he'd take it over the hill to one of the Tanners in Llangennith, the weavers, to make it into cloth for him. I remember one fellow in the village, he made a thing of collecting all the wool he could find, and he'd say: ''A shilling saved is a shilling earned, boy''. That's how they looked upon life.

What you've never had you've never missed, I know, and their vision of life was a narrow one, but in those days there wasn't a lot of pleasure in life. A lot of hardship. A lot of people were cold for one thing. Old people felt the cold then just as keenly as they feel it today. They just lived on top of the fire. The industrious ones picked wreckwood from the beach, some saved up for a bit of coal. With a wife and family to keep if you're earning nine or ten shillings a week, there's little left for coal. So most would buy a little coal, but relied a tremendous amount on driftwood and what we called ''smitty sticks''. They were the charred branches of a furze bush, you'd wait a year after it had been burned, then you can pull the sticks out of the ground. The best thing to burn that ever was. But you'd be lucky to find many left after the farmer had got hold of his own to bake his bread. A big heat for baking they gave off, and it didn't matter how wet they were, they'd dry off in the heat after the baking. The usual rule was that you didn't bake this week until you had sticks ready to put in the oven for next week.

If we wanted coal we'd have to go over to Crofty, ten miles or more, it was a day's job, that, bringing back six or seven hundredweights. Most of the carts had no brake, so on the hills you took a chance, some horses didn't like it at all. If you had a brake you could bring more, of course. One fellow devised a sort of anchor for the wheel, so you could make the cart slide down the hill like a sledge. 'Twas a bad job in my day. But for my mother it was even worse. A sailing ship would bring a load into the pill at Llanmadog, and someone would go with a donkey and fetch back not more than a hundredweight. That was a tedious job if you like.

For lighting in my young days some people would make their own candles, from mutton fat, or later from lumps of 'taller' (tallow) that came ashore, melt it down and put in a bit of string for a wick. But mostly it was an oil-lamp on the table downstairs, candles in the bedroom; the lamp was only allowed upstairs if you were ill in bed, or had a bad cold. Mother would put the lamp on the washstand an hour or two before we went to bed, shut all the doors, and this would warm up the room. Same with the chapel, all lit by lamps, so you never needed heating there, the lamps would be lit an hour before service in the winter, nine lamps, one over the piano and one each side of the pulpit, and once the people were in,—mind you it was full in those days—it was almost too warm. The cleaner was paid a pound a year to clean and light the lamps.

Sheep were often turned into a field after seed had been sown. I have heard it said that this was an ancient way of treading the seed into the ground, but in my view it was not so much that as to keep back the weeds. If you sowed grain in spring weather it would be up in a week, and if it was a weedy field and you didn't have week-killer, you might turn the sheep into it, and they would trample it over. You could put quite a big flock into two acres, say. They'd eat around the hedges and they'd walk over the field, and they'd chop all this small weed into the ground, you see. No better way of killing the weeds. Same thing with the swedes, no weeds will grow if sheep have been in on it. And if you see a good meadow, where the sheep have grazed for years, you won't find any weed in it. The sharp feet of the sheep will kill even the daisies and buttercups. Anyway, if they did eat the young wheat it wouldn't matter at all—it strengthens the growing shoots to be cut back. It's a good way of keeping down the charlock, too. Charlock will choke a field of corn. He'll keep on growing, that stuff.

After the limestone trade faded out, about 1890, the population of the village went down. For example, in 1801 there were 158, fifty years later 367, then by 1911 numbers had dropped to 246. By then, too, shipping had opened up the possibilities of emigrating. Whole families went to Canada, South Africa and Australia. One grandson has just been back to visit the family home. He told me about a little community they had founded in Calgary. The first thing they did was build a wooden chapel—they were Methodists with us here before they left. Some of the sons came home and married local girls, took them back with them. There was quite a recruitment for this "wonderful life in the colonies", a travel agent would come down from Swansea from time to time and hold a meeting, ask for volunteers.

If anyone went to Swansea to look for a job, which was the only thing up to then, the name of George Richards would be sure to crop up. He was the Head Postmaster at Swansea, a Gower man, very partial to his own people, and it was always said that if you went to see George Richards and took him a bag of potatoes, you'd get a job at the Post Office. There was a lot of truth in that. I don't know about the taters, but a whole lot of Gower men landed up in the Post Office, at least four of my uncles had jobs there.

Another good thing to be able to do was drive a horse and cart. It was like being a lorry driver today. All the builders, for example, would have their horse and cart. As a country boy you'd get that sort of job easily, no trouble, carrying sand from the beach, that sort of thing. Or there was the Police, and some boys and girls went to the big stores in Swansea and lived in. They did well for themselves usually. Other girls went as maids in private houses. There wasn't a lot of choice then. But now of course there's no limit.

Up to the eighteen nineties it was farming or quarrying, if

you stayed in the village. It started of course with the burning of the limestone to get lime for the fields. Soil on the limestone is short of lime, you see, because the good drainage takes it away. So they burned the stone in the kilns. But why so many kilns, that's what puzzled me? I can remember thirteen kilns on this bit of coast, and I thought, they can't need all that lime for the few farms in this parish. But an old fellow told me that way back, they first of all exported this burned lime, mostly across the Bristol Channel. And if you notice it, a lime-kiln usually has been built close to the sea, where a sailing ship could float into a cove to load. There's always a handy gully or cove where they could run a chute down into the hold. I mean if they simply wanted lime for themselves, they could have burned it near the top of the cliff, where horses could have carted it away. They'd get the stone from the cliffs, and plenty of wood from the beach. To light the kiln they'd put small sticks, then a layer of coal, a layer of sticks and a layer of coal and so on, and this would burn slowly, for about six days. Then they covered the top with stones, then a few more layers of sticks and coal. I think the exporting of lime itself died out about 1820. Then the major quarrying started, which provided the stone itself for export. And that went on until about 1890, a well paid job while it lasted.

To work a quarry was considered a great privilege. Sometimes it was granted by Mr Talbot as a wedding present to the son of an old tenant, and was highly valued. Stones were needed not only for lime burning but also for walls and the making and repair of roads. Some men were occupied all the year round in breaking stones for the roads.

Before 1910 the quarrymen used an iron bar about six feet long, with a cannon ball halfway down to add extra weight. A hole would be drilled by hand, water being used to keep the head of the bar cool and soften the stone. It would take about a day and a half to drill fifteen to eighteen inches, then the hole would be filled with gunpowder that they carried in a cow's horn slung across the shoulder. They'd then fuse it and blow out a couple of tons of rock. Sledges would be used to break up the big stones and the smaller ones would then be carted to points along the road where they would be broken smaller, usually egg-sized, a very tedious task, but I found it fascinating to watch. The men used hammers with handles of hazel wood, which would resist the vibration. Then they would heap them very neatly under the hedge where they could be measured and paid for by the square yard.

In 1910, when the roads were widened, a donkey engine became available, and a patent drill that could make the holes in a fraction of the time.

The last quarry that was worked was the one at the top of Mewslade Valley.

The main quarries in Rhossili were under the cliffs between Kitchen (corner) and Hocking Hole. A quarryman would have his own 'quar', with a loading bench below to stack his stones. This whole pitch was known as a 'flot quar' (floating quarry) and we still speak today of the parts of the cliff known as 'George Bowen's flot quar' or 'Syd Williams's flot quar'. The men would blast the stones from the cliffs and break them up to the right size, then the women shifted them away, rolled them down against a sort of buttress at the bottom and stacked them neatly ready for loading. The 'shifters' were usually relatives of the quarryman. The women wore canvas skirts and thick leather gloves and they had a very hard and dirty job.

The ships would have to wait for fine weather to cross the water and when two or three arrived by the same tide runners would go round the parish hiring 'heavers', who would help load the boats. Heavers were paid two shillings a tide, and had to watch the tide carefully, since only at high water did the boats rise up high enough to the stacked stones. They would work in a human chain, passing the stones along a line to trimmers, who were expert at the job. Very few women could hold their own in this human chain. A ship would hold about ninety tons, so you can imagine. Two shillings doesn't seem a lot for this, but that was what you'd get for a whole day's work on a farm, and this was an extra to that. The last ship was loaded in 1889, from George Bowen's flot quar, and if you know where to look you can see today a load of stones stacked up for a vessel that never came. It was mostly a summer trade, and in the winter a number of men joined the oyster boats at Porteynon and Mumbles, others signed on coasters for short trips, or did a trip to 'foreign parts', to return to tell of the wonders of the world "t'other side of Pyle Well" as they used to say. In my young days nearly all the older men had 'bin to sea' when they were younger. I remember Billy Jones telling us he had called in a place in Africa where the men *and* the women still lived like in the Garden of Eden. Shocking it was, he said, and he thought we should send out more missionaries. The 'old salts' continued to wear a sailor's blue 'gansey' and a poke cap, to show their superior experience.

In those days, too, we used to have the pleasure steamer calling here on its way from Swansea to Tenby. It would pull in round Worms Head as close to Kitchen Corner as possible, then you could pick up a small boat and be rowed out to the ship, which had less draught of course than the one they use today. Then she'd drop you off again in the evening. But you couldn't do it only on a fine day. There was no need to book, of course, in those days, the ship would call in at Porteynon and here in the hope of picking up a dozen passengers. If it was rough coming back, you could be taken all the way to Swansea, and have to walk home! Shanks pony, after a rough passage! The story is told of one fellow, on his way home, it was too rough to drop him off here, and he was so sick, he said: "Don't you bother, I'm not going any further, just throw me overboard here and let me drown."

But the coast round here has been cruel to shipping, and the sea hasn't had the same effect on the village as it has had in Porteynon. Except perhaps in the catching of crabs and lobsters. This didn't become much of an industry, though, until about 1880. Then with the horse buses going every week into Swansea, it was possible to sell in the town. One fellow I knew would catch anything from thirty to sixty crabs in a day, with a spring tide. And he'd never have any trouble in getting rid of them all, all sold, no trouble tuppence each, penny for the small ones. That surprises me now, because when I catch a few dozen these days, I've got a job to give them away, I even dress them first, too.

There used to be about nine regular crabbers in the village, and each one would have a 'right' to his own crabbing ground, the coast from Paviland to the Worm was divided up to give each a stretch, and woe betide anyone who poached on another's territory. And when one man died another of his family would take it over. But by about fifty years ago it became anybody's ground, though two notable characters used to get most of the crabs. There was Johnny Beynon, who was shown the holes by his grandfather, and Margret Ann (Mrs Beynon). She became an expert at the job, she wore men's hobnailed boots, no stockings, a bathing costume, with an old dress pulled over it, and she'd wade out into the gulleys up to her waist. She sold her catch twice a week in Swansea Market, but Johnny sold his around the village, and never got enough to meet the demand then. He sold his small ones (about five inches long) for 4d, and the very biggest for 1/- each.

I've enjoyed crabbing all my life. The old crabmen taught me the holes. Trouble was, they usually got there before me. Except on the north side of the Worm. Only three of us could get down there. But that was the place where you could catch as much as you could lift up. It was a dangerous spot, mind, but I wasn't bothered about heights. The best crabcrooks used to be made from the rib of a scythe blade, I've still got mine, and I've got an old scythe to make another next year. It's stiff you see, made of hardened steel, so you can feel the crab better. And for the best handle to the crabcrook we used a discarded rocket pole. After they fired a rocket, there was a special pole, about ten foot long for the knotted rope, which was ejected. It was of no use any more, so after every rocket practice there was a spare crabcrook handle. If you got to it first! I've always used one, the last one I had for about ten years, so I said recently to one of the rocket crew, "Next rocket practice, get me a pole". He laughed and said, "They're gone years ago, boy. It's a steel rod now". So that was that. But I had a bit of luck, my grandson found me a nice long bamboo cane near the beach, and it suits me fine. Another one of mine came from a roll of carpet, so now I've got three spare ones.

Another occupation in itself used to be making laverbread (or 'lowa' as it was known locally). The women picked the weed, and the whole thing was a tedious and hard job, picking it and boiling it, then they'd chop it up finely with a cleaver on an oak slab they'd picked up on the beach, chop, chop, chop, chop, chop, for hours on end they'd be doing this. I remember an old woman, living up on the hill and when we were in school, we'd go up and help her chop, chop, chop. Of course we used to enjoy this, chopping away at this great heap of laverbread, we'd chop it up fine for her and she'd give us a halfpenny. The laverbread pickers didn't have fixed pitches for picking like the crabbers did. They'd vie with each other to find the best and cleanest weed. There was one spot, a patch of rocks well out in the middle of Rhossili Bay, not exposed today, called the Cow and Calf, and the women would be waiting to get out there, prolific crop of weed on it usually. And there is an old story of two women of the village who had a real set-to just here. Someone wrote a verse about it and it's been handed down since it happened, oh, surely a hundred years ago:

> There was a mighty battle
> Fought on Rhossili sands,
> Between the Queen of Sheba (Sarah Bowen)
> and the Doctoress of our land.
> The Doctoress's name was Betty (Ace),
> She was of a savage race,
> She wore a dreadful countenance,
> The daughter of Sam Ace.
> The Queen was tall and fiery
> And fought like Higgie's cat (Leppintrileps),
> But what she gained in inches
> Was lost by too much fat.
> The Doctoress poked and parried,
> The Queen she used her nails.
> The battle raged with fury
> As each the other shook,
> The Doctoress punched the harder,
> But Sheba used her hook.
> So when the contest ended

'Twas fairly plain to see
That neither had asked for mercy:
For one was buying plaster,
And t'other couldn't see.

With very few exceptions all the farms in the parish were
owned by the Penrice Estate and I must admit that relations
between tenant and landlord have been on the whole kind and
cordial. Rents were cheap, tenancy was permanent—if you
behaved yourself!—and there wasn't any interference in
methods of agriculture. The first landlord I remember was Miss
Talbot. She was the daughter of Mr C. M. Talbot, who was the
Liberal M.P. for Glamorgan for fifty years. They say that the
only time he spoke in the House was to ask someone to open
the window. But his influence here was enormous. He was a
Liberal, so it wasn't so bad as if he had been a Conservative. On
the other hand, when the Labour Party started up and grew, the
Estate became very wary—for example, when they granted the
village land for a village hall, in 1924—Lady Blytheswood was
the landlord by then—she made a proviso that no political
meetings were to be held in it! Because Gower had by then a
Labour M.P., you see, that was a terrible thing. But we really
kicked about that and the condition was squashed. I mean,
where else could we hold a meeting anyway?

There were differences, of course, between tenant and landlord but they were usually settled at the annual Leet Court.
Here the law of custom prevailed over the law of the statute
book. Say two farmers disagreed about a fence. Now the law of
the land says that you must keep your stock within your boundaries, not that I must keep them out of my land. But the law of
custom, as it was and still is in Gower, says that it is my duty to
keep cattle *out* of my confines. I can well remember having a
quarrel with a neighbour about a fence, and the Penrice steward
at the time, Hopkin Llewelyn Pritchard, eighteen stone, standing about six foot seven and carrying a big alpenstock, came
down and looked at the problem and he cried out: "Dammit,
man, we don't go by law here, you know, we go by custom! And
so you keep your fence proper! Then this man's cattle won't get

in!'' And that was the 'Law'! Among the customs the Talbot family used to keep up was their 'Worms Head mutton'. They would put a flock of wethers out there to graze and would kill one of them every week throughout the winter—they'd have lamb in the summer, I suppose—because lamb becomes mutton after August. One farmer had the job of collecting one of these sheep every Tuesday, and it would be taken to Penrice by a servant, in a trap. It would be killed at Penrice, and enjoyed by the family, if they were in residence, or sent to them wherever they were in a special box made for the purpose. Oh, the old people swore there was nothing like Worms Head mutton, they used to think the salt grass gave it a special flavour. I believe it was a fallacy, mind, but all right, perhaps it did.

For some reason too they ordered that all sheep on the estate should be sheared by a certain date. Then they'd send round servants on ponies with dogs to round up any that hadn't been sheared. I know one farmer was fined in the Leet Court for this.

Mind, this sort of autocracy did cause reaction. Many people became quite bitter, though most took it for granted. Any animosity, though, showed itself, not so much between the tenant and the landlord as between the Church and the Chapel in the village. They could do nothing about having a landlord, they had to accept that. But they resented the imposition of the tithe on the land, and also the siding of the landlord with the Church. The Church was at fault too, they were all county stock, and hand in glove with the gentry. Miss Talbot used to invite all us children to tea and games at the Castle once a year. All transport free, and we were allowed to roam around the park, and pick chestnuts, and look at the gardens. Organised games on the front lawn, with all the servants looking on from the vast number of windows. Then tea in the servants' hall, served by real butlers, then after singing a grace, back to the front lawn for a concert for Miss Talbot. The parson was always there, so he gave a speech of thanks, and then the head butler would hand out a big bun to every child to take home, and, this is what I was getting at, every child from the Church Sunday School would get a length of cloth for a dress or a suit—but the chapel child would get nothing. A little thing, but it meant a lot.

Gower Show, Penrice Park, 1934.

Again, when the family went down to Oxwich Bay to picnic and bathe, they went down in a carriage with servants, and they made sure they had the beach to themselves. They owned the dunes, you see, and the beach above high water mark, so they could order anyone off. Which they did, too, if they had a family party there. And that is the real reason why Gower remained so unspoiled, not through any positive policy of conserving it. They simply owned it, they were conservative, and they didn't allow any changes. Fortunately the industrial revolution didn't touch Gower, the Estate wouldn't have allowed it anyway. Anything that encroached on their game rights or their access to the beaches—they soon put a stop to it. So we're sort of benefiting today from the restrictions that Penrice put on us in the past.

But all that changed when the Estate was broken up in 1950. That was the most important change ever in the farming life of this part of Gower. You see, during the Second World War Lady Blytheswood transferred the estate to her daughter, Mrs Methuen Campbell, to avoid paying crippling death duties. Lady Blytheswood was about 70, and her daughter relatively young. But in 1948 lo and behold the daughter died, and Lady Blytheswood was still alive. So the death duties had to be paid anyway. And the estate had to be sold, no alternative really. They sent a letter to every sitting tenant offering the farm to him at a stated price. That had to be low, because in 1947 the Labour Government had passed the security of Tenure Act. Rents couldn't be raised, and now no farmer could be ejected. So now they were offered their land for roughly £50 an acre. No bartering. Now it's £500. I mean, that wasn't a sale, it was a gift. A farm of thirty acres for £1,500. Even in those days it was a generous price. Some were foolish enough not to buy, and cottages were on sale then for £300 or £400. Pitton Mill, for instance, that fetched £425, and recently it was sold for £7,500. And a farm near here, that was bought at the time for about £4,000, it was sold a few months ago for £110,000.

The difference this made to farming was tremendous. No trouble now to borrow from a bank and build up your own little estate. And there were no game rights any more. Everyone could carry on in complete freedom and independence. But it was a lucky accident that that Act had been passed, or the whole history of this community would have been different. Buildings went up, and the farms increased in value and efficiency. Then in 1951 this Act was cancelled and the Government began to give grants to farmers to help things like drainage and improve buildings. Grants sometimes of up to 60%. Farmers had it almost all their own way. That's why Evans the Minister of Agriculture said they were 'feather-bedded' by two Governments.

And now of course, politically speaking, we began to look after landlords rather than tenant farmers. It was during the Second World War the foundations were laid. If your farm was under 100 acres you didn't pay income tax. You could sell £2,000 worth of cabbage and not pay a penny tax. Even a larger farm paid only on acreage. No accounting was necessary.

I was fortunate enough to have a very good village school teacher. She actually had a degree and had come to live near here to look after her father who was a Congregational minister. She was really dedicated. She taught me things like Algebra and Latin and French prefixes that I still find useful today. And Geometry. She was very keen on grammar, too, (which, as you can see, I'm not too fussy about!) but she left when I was coming to thirteen, and we had a new teacher who wasn't a patch on old Miss Edwards. She was really a tremendous influence on the formative years of my life. And I wasn't the only one. One thing she instilled into me was a desire to learn, so all my life I've read all I can, and enjoyed the W.E.A. and extra-mural classes in the village. She got me to sit the exam for the secondary school, and I passed it, but the expense of going there was too much for my mother, me having to lodge for a week in Gowerton and pay a fee. I can only think of three who went in my time, and one came back as headmistress of the village school.

The first school in the village I can find a record of was held in a stall belonging to the Ship Inn, opposite it and still used as a stable. In the eighteen-fifties the teacher was an old village woman, then about 1860 the school was moved to what was the village almshouse, occupied by four or five people on parish relief. It was then a thatched cottage with partition walls, the first floor was removed and it left one big room with an earth floor. It was staffed by anyone who was prepared to sit with the children. About 1868 it was an old woman named Peggy Williams. She sat at a table in the middle of the room, and the pupils sat on benches around the walls. She darned or knitted the whole time, unless a child wanted to ask a question. If it was a difficult one she couldn't answer. Her wages were about nine shillings a week, paid by Mr Talbot, and the parson would come twice a week to give a scripture lesson. Attendance was not compulsory, of course, so children only went when it suited their parents. Mr Talbot would visit the school from time to time, driven in a carriage attended by two footmen. The next teacher, Will Taylor, seems to have been of the same educational standard. An old villager told me he asked him once to help him with a sum. He pondered for a long time and failed to find an answer and then he said: "Well, never thee mind, George, if both of us can't do it, it won't matter". He had been a miller, but had left his wife to look after the mill so that he could be the teacher. But he still killed the local pigs, and closed the school for the day if he had a pig to kill. Still, because he couldn't knit or darn the children got more attention. Some of the village children, if they could afford sevenpence a week, were sent to Porteynon School, where there was a very good teacher, a Mr George, grandfather of Professor Neville George formerly of Glasgow University.

In 1881 the School came under the care of the School Board, and the attendance improved, even if the educational standards didn't. Appointments were made now by the Board, and not by Mr Talbot. Various teachers came and went, and when I went to school, in 1903, it was Mr Henderson. He had taken over from Dirty Dick, as they called Mr Dick Hughes. He was a small man, very severe on the pupils. He caned one girl so hard she was left with a weal on her hand, so her mother one day caught him and put him on his back in the gutter. For which she was fined ten shillings. By the time I knew Mr Henderson he had become slovenly, and was a lazy drunkard, spending his time raging at the children or roasting chestnuts in the fire. He got dismissed in 1905 and the next time I saw him about fifteen years later he was in the Swansea Workhouse. Then we got Miss Edwards, and she brought something that had never happened before.

Elections to the School Board which were held every three years were quite an event in the village. Right from the beginning, in 1881, they were a battle between the Church and the Methodists for power. Each would nominate three candidates and there were five seats. Every elector had five votes and these could be distributed as he or she liked. The Church people always managed to get the parson on, by a big margin but by doing so their other two candidates were low on the list. But the Wesleyans were very clever and methodical, and ensured that their three would get an equal number of votes by 'plonking'. The faithful members would each plonk and give their five votes to one candidate or the other. In this way they could get a majority almost every time. Parson Lucas wasn't really interested, so there wasn't any serious animosity until Parson Hughes took his place. He was a fighter and was determined to swing the majority. The gloves were off in earnest. But again the Church mismanaged the campaign and Parson got all the votes. The cunning of the nonconformists had won again. But the two things stuck in their throats all the time: the compulsory religious instruction by the parson, and of course, the tithe that was added to the rent, and then paid to the Church. Oh, to my old grandfather there never was such an imposition! He would never touch his hat to the parson, never, never. The climax of the battle came in 1902, when the duties of School Boards came to an end, and it had to be decided by the parish whether to hand over the school to the County Education Authority, or make it a Church School. About the biggest controversy the village has never known, I should think! Parson Hughes was determined to win this time. But to the puritan mind nothing could be more terrible. But again Pastor Hughes got most of the Church votes, and when the result was announced at the school, he was heard to say: "And those damned Wesleyans have won again"!

I was proud of one thing: I was the first Socialist to be made a magistrate in Gower. And the first who wasn't a freemason. I must say the years I was on the bench were very interesting, you felt you were doing something that mattered. For seven years I was chairman of the Juvenile Bench, and it taught me a lot. Does it matter, do you think, whether you put him or her in the care of the local authority? I know now that it does matter, very, very much. Your decision one way or the other can affect their lives radically.

When I was young the lawyer of the parish was Sam Bevan. He was the wise man. And he *was* wise. I don't know what he knew about the law, but he kept law books in the house and read them. And if there was a dispute, ''We'll ask Sam Bevan'', they'd say. And they'd accept his ruling. Besides that, he read the paper. He had a paper posted to him once a week, and he would read it out on a Saturday morning to a gathering of those interested. And when my uncle went away to London, he used to send my father a paper. Guess what it was! The News of the World! Sam Bevan was a cooper by trade and he spent a lot of time at Penrice Castle, making water butts for the Estate, and any farmer who needed one could get one. He was as bald as a bladder, but he must have been very clever, because he could do mathematical problems and all that. People said he was lazy, but if he was an intellectual, that was understandable; he appeared to be lazy, when he was just reading, or thinking. In his younger days he was the arch-schemer for the nonconformists in the School Board elections, but later on he became a church-warden.

Then there was the two cobblers. One was George Bevan, un-educated, almost illiterate. But he had to be the first with any-thing new. He bought the first mowing machine, to cut the hay, and a reaper and binder, I don't know where he got the money from. William Morgan was the other cobbler. He brought up a very large family, worked hard all day for six days in the week, and in the evenings he'd walk miles delivering the boots he had repaired and picking up boots to repair. He was the first, too, to buy a noted watch, a silver Samuel's watch for a pound, and he always had the correct time. Coming out of chapel we used to

Gower Magistrates 1967-1968.
(back row, left to right) Rhodri Harris (Mag. Clerk), George Richards, Mrs. M. Davies,
Mrs. C. Saunders, Mrs. M. D. Rott, G. Grove, Jack Bevan (Vice Chairman);
(front row, left to right) Sir Cenydd Traherne, George Tucker (Chairman), Richard John,
John Richards.

ask him: "What time is it, Mr Morgan?". And he'd pull out his watch and he'd say: "Seven and a half minutes past twelve". It was a novelty really to get the time correct to a minute or two, because you see there is no clock in the village, the only way you could have the time was by the sundial on the church gateway. The only other sure way, was, when the sun was shining, to go to look at the old coastguard station, which is built exactly due north to south, and at twelve o'clock the shadow of the chimney should be halfway over each side of the crest of the roof. We went by that. And I do now, if I go crabbing at midday. Anyway, it didn't use to be all that important. Time didn't matter so much then.

We used to have women characters in the village, too. These were the 'doctoresses'. For about forty years Betty Ace (she was in the fight on the sands) acted as an unqualified G.P. She collected herbs and boiled them and steamed them and crushed them, and the villagers thought that what she didn't know about humans and beasts was not worth knowing. She supplied ointments and medicines for all kinds of ailments. One old man told me she had cured him of jaundice in a week. He believed the faith that people had in her was fully justified. They would never call the doctor down if she was looking after them. If they died, they died, and that was the end of it. Mrs Chalk then came after her, she was the midwife for every child in two or three parishes. For about thirty years. She would stride off over the fields and the hills in her hob-nailed boots and still the doctor was not called unless she thought he was needed. It meant seven visits to the mother and child after the confinement, and she got seven shillings from a farmworker's wife and ten shillings from a farmer's wife, with five shillings extra if the doctor wasn't called. She'd walk miles, too, to lay out the dead, and for this she'd get five shillings. Her daughter-in-law, also a Mrs Chalk, took over from her when she died and carried on in the same way, but by then the doctor had to be present at every case.

Getting a doctor was quite a business. You had to walk or ride a horse seven miles to tell him, then he'd have to get to your place somehow. There'd be a day lost, whatever.

I never remember a doctor calling at our house. My mother was our doctor: feet in mustard and water for a cold, and goose grease on the chest, flour and water with a pinch of saltpetre for a good sweat, and for something more serious the midwife would be called in. Neither she nor my mother knew anything about temperatures or medicines, except senna tea, but we survived somehow. One famous remedy, for a festered finger, was the fat bacon poultice. The bacon would be hanging up in the kitchen and you'd leave the fat end to grow mould on it, we wouldn't cut that off. Then when it was needed you'd scrape the mould off with your fingernail, put it onto a strip of linen, and put it on your festering cut, and leave it. This was nothing more or less than a form of penicillin, of course, as we've learned by now.

This has always been known as 'wreckers' coast', and wrecks have played quite a part in the life of the parish. People still talk about 'going wrecking', though now all they're doing is collecting a few sticks from the beach, very little real 'wreck-wood' about today. But not so long ago a wreck would be quite a bonus. By the time the customs were notified, and had come down from Swansea, the wreck would be stripped, oh yes, that's common knowledge. And the cargo, well, you could usually buy that cheap anyway. In my young days all the ladders were made from masts, best the thin masts of a sailing ship. One boat, the *Samuel*, come in at the Sound, high up, and she was loaded with coal. Well, you can imagine. It was carted up above high water mark and the parish had free or cheap coal for a very long time. Only it was small stuff, we had to mix it with clay to burn it. Then if you got hold of a cask of spirits, you could sell that to the pubs, you see, if you were a teetotaller yourself.

Before the coastguard was stationed here, there was a man appointed by the Customs to keep an eye on any wreck that happened. And the story is that a boat had been wrecked, so he set off to Swansea to report it, eighteen miles walk. Well, after going three or four miles he realised that by the time he got to Swansea all the 'prog' would have disappeared, and he'd get

Men with winecask, Worm's Head, 1938.

nothing of it. So back he came, and made sure of a share for himself before he went off to report it.

The best wrecking I knew—wood, that is,—was in the First
World War. There must have been a timber ship loaded with
these joists—seven by two they were—and they were coming in
at all places and all times and every inch of the coast was thick
with them, the coastguards had no chance. I remember my
uncle coming in and telling us they were coming in 'like match-
sticks'. So after dark we went down to collect what we could.
We got a lot in, but oh dear, dear, after a few hours we were so
exhausted trying to carry them up the cliffs. Suddenly we saw a
coastguard coming along in the half light, so we had to lie down
in the furze and wait for him to go by. I remember my uncle saying: "For God's sake, boy, don't shout", he said, "He'll die of
fright". We left a lot of the timber in the fields, then next morning we got a cart and got them up. But it was a great shame, the
sea came up and washed so much out again. I've been making a
list of the wrecks that have come in in this parish, but I'm
relying entirely on the memories of the old people, so I may

have missed one or two. But two that can still be seen in remains are:

1887 *Helvetia*

She was anchored off Mumbles but had to cut adrift because of heavy wind and sea. She drifted ashore in Rhossili Bay to the village side of the Old Parsonage. She was a wooden ship, plated up to the water-line with copper sheets, she also had a copper keel. My father bought her, and stripped her of everything useful before she settled in the sand. Our own farmhouse kitchen was floored with her deck-boards. The crew were saved because the ship stood upright in the sand. Her timbers are still to be seen sticking out of the sands of the Bay.

1894 *Verani*

An iron sailing ship, a Norwegian on her maiden voyage, came in under the Rhossili cliffs. The rocket crew found it impossible to get a line across from the cliff top so they used a human chain from the beach and all the crew were saved, including the captain's wife, with her six months old baby. Remains of the ship can still be seen at low water, right under the cliffs.

The roads as I remember them as a boy over seventy years ago had not changed probably for centuries. There is only one 'main' road leading out of the village, in the direction of Swansea, and that used to be a narrow cart road, about ten feet wide, with high hedges each side. The surface was rough, cut up with horses' hooves in the centre and cart tracks at the sides. Occasionally the pits were filled with egg-sized stones and the sides were hacked in to make it more level but if it was muddy, well, the mud came over your boots. About 1908 we saw the first steam roller, and that made it possible to sweep away the mud sometimes.

The village is a dead end of course, so there is no through traffic. Up to 1870 there was no organized transport. It was horse and cart or just horseback, or, as many of the crabbers and laverbread-pickers had to, it was shanks' pony, with a basket on the head. Thirty-six miles, to Swansea and back. A small one-horse brake started a regular weekly service (William Button,

Pitton Cross) in the eighteen eighties, and two years later he got
a two-horse bus big enough to take everybody and everything. A
Wednesday and Saturday service was started in the nineties,
and—great sensation—the Taylors started a motor bus going in
on Mondays, Wednesdays, Fridays and Saturdays (twice!). That
was in 1920.

But from the early days the busman was an important and
prosperous man. Farmers and their wives would give him all
kinds of orders: ploughshares from Griffiths, boots from
Oliver's, pills from Bevan's, a trouser for our Johnny, a dozen
salt herrings from Chappell's, a piece of calico from Lewis's.
There was a story of an old fellow giving an order for a piece of
calico. He couldn't remember how much, so after much head-
scratching he murmured: "Oh, enough to make our Mary a pair
of drawers." He would put all this down, then be paid on his
return, or he would have been given a rabbit or two, or some
eggs, or half a bag of potatoes, something that he could sell.

When the motor bus started I well remember the arguments
for and against. "Anyway, we'll get to Swansea in less than two
hours", "You'll see, we'll break down and have to spend the
night on the road", "It won't be safe to drive cattle on the road
now", "No more walking up hills"? "We'll be gassed by the
fumes and choked by the dust". And so it went on. They did kill
a cow in the first week, and I suppose all the other things happened too. Anyway, soon we had a daily service. But children
had to be kept off the road when the bus was due. Horses in the
fields had to be held and turned round. Hedges got heavy with
white limestone dust and we got choked with it, so that the rain
coming to "quot the pilm" was always very welcome. The first
bus was an open tourer with a flapping hood, a great thrill to the
youngsters, then we had one with a fixed canvas hood and
adjustable sides, then came the enclosed bus, with a ladder at
the back, to get parcels and passengers on to the roof. I always
went up there, with a tarpaulin to protect us from the weather
and a low rail to stop us falling off.

In 1910 the council decided to widen the road, and it was
made its present width in eighteen months. Unfortunately they
removed a dozen or so lovely trees in the centre of the village

and did nothing to replace them. The new road had a low hedge on the south side, so it dried off more quickly, and the greater width meant that carts didn't have to use each other's tracks.

When I see the cars streaming down in summertime now on the smooth macadamed roadway, no ruts, no potholes, I wonder if its been an improvement!

Mr Hughes was the first Rector I remember. He had succeeded Mr Lucas who died here in 1898. Mr Lucas was also vicar of Llangennith and used to walk, or ride on horseback or pony trap to cover his parishes.

Many are the tales of parson Lucas and his autocratic ways. He had a small farm of twelve acres of glebe land around his Parsonage in the middle of Rhossili Bay and here he employed one or

two men, as well as two maids in the house. It is said that he only spoke to them once a day, to give them orders at nine o'clock in the morning. It seems he sacked one man because he did not touch his cap as he passed by the study window. Even if he met the postman in the village he would insist that he walked all the way down to the parsonage with him, not exchanging a word. The postman was a nonconformist, I understand. Every parishioner was expected to lift his cap and address him as "sir", which really stuck in the throats of the villagers. After preaching in church he would leave the church with the congregation still seated and walk home without once even wishing anyone a good-day.

But for all this odd behaviour he was held with reverence by many of the people. He was generous to the poor and sick and looked upon himself as a parish priest.

Mr Hughes, who came next, was a bachelor, an excellent preacher and was very interested in singing, as well as the social life of the parish. Trouble with him was he had a violent temper. I once saw him stop the organist and the choir in the middle of a hymn and thunder at them: "You're going through this like a lot of little donkeys". That was the last time the organist or the choir set foot in the church. With a village already divided into two camps, he didn't help matters.

Mr Scudamore came in 1921. Much more docile and placid than any of his predecessors; he was deeply religious, but his belief in High Church doctrine and ritual—incense was burned in the church and sprayed at matins—created a stir in the church-goers and his congregation got smaller and smaller. We nonconformists used to go to church simply to see this 'catholic performance' as we called it. But still he was never known to do or say anything unkind, and I think he could claim more friends in the parish than his two predecessors. Perhaps that is a greater tribute than church membership. The Church Commissioners sold the Old Parsonage in 1926 and Rhossili and Llangennith became separate church parishes.

Before 1820 the Methodist services were held in the kitchen of Great Pitton Farm, then a small chapel was built in the garden, and the present chapel on the main road was built in

1886 by William Richards, Harepits, for £150. Stones and sand were carted free by local farmers and members of other chapels in the circuit. The stones were dug out of Rhossili Hill by George Bowen. The new chapel was opened with a great gathering in 1886, but the celebration was marred by a worldly counter-attraction—the one and only visit to the village of a 'wild beast show'!

In those days the local preachers had to take a horse or walk each Sunday to fill their appointments. One of them told me once he often walked to Oxwich Green to take a morning service, then walked again 'over the hill' to Llangennith, to take an evening one. Chapel in those days made a deep impression on the life of the parish. I think its stern puritan outlook, and its condemnation of drink, gambling, and dancing, soured rather than sweetened the life of the young people, just when a little tolerance would have helped. But what with prayer meetings, Band of Hope and choir practice, it did keep us together. One event that has died out was the Blue Ribbon Tea in February. This was a temperance do, when all the children sang or recited about the evils of strong drink. Like the verse that ended: ''The lips that touch liquor shall never touch mine''. We were all pressed into singing the pledge and given a strip of blue ribbon to wear.

Then there was the May Tea, second week in May, an occasion for all the chapels in the circuit to unite and an excuse for new clothes among the young people.

Not a lot left now, except of spiritual fellowship among the faithful band of members, and that is as strong as ever, I'm glad to say.

The Congregational cause at Pilton Green goes back to about 1830, and has had some powerful preachers. One of them is said to have brought tonic solfa to Gower for the first time. In 1930 the Manse was let, and lay preachers kept services going up to the War, and again afterwards, and it still supplies the need of a community otherwise without a place of worship.

The game rights in this parish were held by Colonel Helme of Hill End, and it was the event of the year when he invited all the tenants to Hill End in September or October for a Harvest Supper and Dance.

There was very few pheasants down this end, of course, but no end of partridge in those days, not like now. And if a partridge was shot on your land, he'd give you a shilling—for the field it fell in, not the field it was shot in. We'd regularly get a few shillings for partridges that were shot on someone else's field, especially on one strip that was usually ploughed and didn't shelter the birds. Then he'd give you something for a magpie's egg, threepence I think it was, and sixpence for a magpie's head, and sixpence for a stoat's tail. They were the enemies of game, you see, and good riddance to them. I used to get quite a bit of extra, because I looked out for the magpie's nests, and we shot them and cut off their heads, and we had a dog that could catch stoats, so we'd give all of these to a man who worked at Hill End, Colonel Helme's place, then at Christmastime every year, we'd get payment, in new coins. Quite a little fortune it was.

There were not many magpies to be seen about in those days. Stoats were more of a menace in a way because a stoat will kill a young pheasant. An interesting thing about a stoat is that he doesn't like going through a gateway. He'll come up to it and then look for another way of getting through. So on the Estate, when they were putting up gate-posts, they'd build a little hole for the stoat to go through, a hole about four inches square, like a gutter hole, built of brick, and that's where the keepers would put their gins, to trap the stoats. That's all in the past now, of course.

I only shoot for the pot myself. I can't for the life of me catch a fish that is no good to eat—carp, pike, that sort, I always throw them back. I couldn't shoot a seagull for the same reason. I did shoot a fox once. I was down in the valley one day, with a gun, looking for rabbits. There was a young couple over the other side of the valley, and they shouted across at me: "There's a fox, look! In front of you. In the furze there!" I sent the dog in, and out ran this fox. And I shot. I walked up to him and he was lying there, bleeding. A great big dog fox. And I thought . . . well, well, . . . this doesn't fit you, boy, at all. I know foxes do damage, of course, but . . . Anyway, these youngsters came racing across the valley to see what had happened. And the first thing I said was: "Look what you've blooming well made me do," I said, I was so annoyed with myself. "Why, what's up?", they said. "Well, look at that beautiful animal," I said, "And I've gone and killed him, just look at him". They must have thought I was cracked. Anyway, there we are, he was dead, and that was the end of it. He was my first and I made sure he was my last. I still sort of feel ashamed of it. Because in my heart of hearts I believe in conservation.

FIELD AND PLACE NAMES

The Slent	path leading from Rhossili village up towards top of hill
Resting Bank	rock at bottom of Mewslade Lane with a view down the valley
Gupurra Lane	cart road going east from Gr. Pitton yard
Dead Man's Kiln	Mewslade Valley
Ferny Pit	partly walled in cliff field W. of Ramsgrove
Mine House Corner	above Red Chamber in field. Winch for lead mine
Fiddler's Hay	partly walled-in cliff field W. of Ramsgrove
Sally Bargain	enclosure opposite Pitton Mill
Bunkers Hill	road up hill from Higher Pitton
The Zogs	boggy field, top of Pitton valley
Button Lane	short lane to L. of Sheep Lane
The Bottoms	(or Bevan's Bottoms) where water goes underground near main road at Higher Pitton
Vould	where lime kiln is on cliff between Mewslade and Fall
Aspen Pool	(or Absent Pool) corner near Margam Farm
Kinmoor Lane	road—Roman?—joining Pitton Cross and Rhossili Hill
Little Hill	part of Rhossili Down nearest the village
The Towers	heap of stones on top of Rhossili Hill, removed during World War Two
Hanging Skers	last rock peak on Rhossili Hill nearest Llangennith
Bessie's Meadow	grassy meadow dipping from Hill to Hill End

Harper(s) Street	road above cottages at Higher Pitton
Watch Pool	about 50 yards north of school on hill
The Bank	crossing at Middleton
Lazy Bank	crossing at Pitton
Wrinkle Tor	big rock left of Mewslade valley
Iley	stream 100 yards E. of Old Parsonage. Good drinking water
Rolling Tor	path around first bend of hill on way to the Old Parsonage
Hocking Hole	field next to old quarries on Rhossili cliff
Hock Well	field adjoining Rhossili Down near top
Windy Walls	two thatched cottages north of school. One up one down. One occupied by Granny Hopkins, laverbread picker, the other by George Bevan a shoemaker. No cupboard bed, no stairs, only ladder. But he slept on a bench downstairs and worked at the window. Rent for house and garden was 9d. a week, which he thought was 'exorbitant'.
Purgatory	On hill up from Rhossili. Badly built. Last occupied about 1890.
Talgarths Well	Thatched cottage with two rooms down, one up. Footpath from Middleton to Pitton passed the front door and through the garden.
Peggy's House	Next to Lower Shop in Mewslade Lane. 2 rooms
Hoarstone	Cottage on Bunkers Hill.
Pudley Wharf	Off Pilton Green.
Pitton Mill	Lower than present Mill by about 50 yards. Road ended here. Last occupied by Will Taylor about 1880.
'Bull's Eye'	Beer house in Sheep Lane. Built in corner of garden what is now Riverside Cottage.

WILL JONES

Blacksmith

Born in Reynoldston in 1891

Horses were my life, really. My family used to drive the horse-bus into Swansea, and when I was a boy my father used to haul coal across from Lynch Colliery near Penclawdd. He'd be in front with his horse Charlie, and I'd be behind with old Captain. We'd get ten or twelve hundredweight, buying it at sixpence a bag and putting it in for you at a shilling. Splendid coal it was, too, no dirt in it, good for the smithy, for welding, clean. I remember there was an old chap at the weighbridge, fond of his glass of beer. So we'd buy two pints of pale ale at the brewery at Reynoldston, 6d. for the quart, and take them for him. Then when we'd be chucking in the coal, and he'd be weighing it, he'd say: "Thee's got a bit over today, boy, never mind, go on . . ."

When I was seventeen, what I wanted to learn was shoeing, so I started with a man in Swansea, a Devonshire fellow, and by damn it nearly killed me. We were at it early, five o'clock in the morning, and we had to shoe eight to ten horses before breakfast. They had to be got ready, you see, for the men to start work. About half an hour a horse was the limit. But my hands got all skinned, my legs were all in, and the doctor ordered me home. And I couldn't see straight, I'd walk into the garden hedge instead of going round.

But then came the Army. I joined up the day before my twenty-fourth birthday. When I got the chance I went on a course for R.S.S., that's Regimental Shoeing Smith. I come out on top and I was made a Farrier Sergeant. I sent for my sweetheart and we got married, in Northampton. I was taken off one draft after another, because I was too handy where I was, training these boys to learn shoeing, twelve at a time,—too many,— you could't learn 'em all. But I got a pound for every one that passed out. I only did cold shoeing with them, that's only picking up any old shoe that fitted and nailing it on. Hot shoeing is starting from the forge. But if you could do cold shoeing, you'd most likely be sent to France. And I had to instruct the officers

"Horses were my life, really."

on the parts of the foot and things . . . where they could drive the
nail in, the centre part, and the frog and the cannon bone, the
two splint bones coming up the side. And when a splint grew
fast to them three bones, the horse got lame, you see, so you had
to blister it, to take the hardness out of it. Or the horse might
get ringbone, right round the top of the coronet, that's the top of
the hoof. Or we'd get a horse with a corn inside the hoof. I used
to cut off the shoe near the corn, but the officers thought I was
daft, and didn't know what I was doing. The tricks you learned
in civvy life you had to be careful with in the Army. Same with
the lampas, that affects the roof of the horse's mouth, bruised
by eating, with their short teeth, so that the roof comes down
over their front teeth. Now I'd burn that with a hot iron, and
then pull it off. Dab it then with iodine or turpentine, take a
horse nail and prick it from both sides and squeeze the blood
out. A handful of salt then and rub it in where I'd burned. I
wasn't allowed to do that in the Army. But I did a bit on the sly,
like. No, they said, feed him with soft food till it gets better. But
that's all bunk. The old horse gets thin, out of condition. I got in

a bit of trouble once, because they found blood in the manger. You had to be a bit of a vet as well, you see. Why, even now people bring their cats and dogs to me.

Funny thing, we used to come across some horses we recognised, from these parts. Requisitioned. The Army was paying exorbitant prices for them. My own horse was Cochyn, bit hard in the mouth she was but she could go. I got her out of the sick lines, and she come from a butcher's cart in Morriston.

In 1917 I was sent to Salonika, with the job of getting the food and ammunition up the line. I had a rough time with the fellows under me there, some of them had 18 years service. But I told them: "If a horse comes down to the forge sound, he must go out sound". We had a portable forge, a little anvil we used to carry around, about a hundredweight. There were still kilts on the barbed wire at Gallipoli, terrible mistake that was. I must say I felt pretty spiteful about the Germans. I mean, if you were a German, I wouldn't let you off. We'd "take care" of you. You wouldn't get the chance to come back at us again. But that's what we were trained for, you see. Built up for it. And to give you extra buck you'd get an extra half pint of rum. A lot of our chaps got killed, our job was to plant ammunition in No Man's Land, ready for us to move on.

In the end I was sent home with malaria, so I set up as a blacksmith in the village here, and there I was for forty years. I enjoyed the life in lots of ways. Shoeing, of course. All the horses around. And the gypsies. Once I shoed a donkey, used for carrying water. But he was so short, I had to dig a pit to get down to his legs, to give me a bit of room to work in. What I'd like to have done was shoe an ox. I found a shoe here in the garden, off an ox. Just the shape of a kidney, with two holes at the toe, that's all. The drovers used to use them. Some horses were very nasty, mind. One of them'd go mad and throw me against the wall and let go at me with his feet just like a boxer. Lucky I knew how to defend myself. Trouble was they used to rear up and land on my toes. I've had bad toenails ever since.

The worse kick I got though was in the Army. Just after I'd had it, in my private parts, I was walking down the street at Northampton, and it wasn't half stinging, when I met the vicar.

"What's the matter, farrier?", he said. "I've had a bad kick vicar". I think he doubted me, there were a lot of nasty things knocking about in them days. "You'd better come back to the vicarage with me", he said. So I did, and he put me on a couch and called his wife. I really was in a hell of a mess, all black and blue, up to my navel. Anyway, his wife seemed to know her way around, and she made a belt of cotton wool and sewed it all up, to keep me from rubbing, you know. Did a grand job. I reported to the M.O. He was drunk, smelling of whisky, but he said, "Nothing broken, thank God . . . huh . . . huh . . . huh . . . Light duty". No guard or pickets, very nice. But by God, I was sore, for a bit.

I learned to defend myself at an early age. There was a boy, from the Homes he was, learning farming, and he used to come to the forge and try to throw me. I got tired of that, so I told him "Now look, next time you do that, I'll put one on yer". So I gave him a black eye. There was boxing in every village then, so there were lots of fellows keen to try me out. I heard one of them say one day . . . I was about eighteen then . . . "Will Jones! A couldn't hit a herring off a bloody gridiron". He come to the forge one day, and he taunted me: "They tell me thee's pretty good with thee hands . . . I'd like to ha' a go at thee". The gloves were hanging up, but his hands were so big he couldn't get them into the gloves, they were just a pair I'd bought in a pawnshop in Swansea. So, nothing to do, I opened an old seaman's chest I kept my shoeing nails in, and there was a pair of old hedging gloves in there, all crinkled and rough, so he put these on. We went outside, to the field behind the forge, sloping up like that and a lot of long dead grass. He went up the slope and come down at me, like a mad bull. He turned and I let him have it. I looked, and he was all covered in blood. I had to get a bucket of water to wash him down. Anyway, that was the end of him. I gave him a beauty, mind. He'd have killed me if I hadn't put him out first pop. I heard he wasn't right, you know. Penny short of a shilling, like.

We used to have great fun at the old boxing booth at Reynoldston, time of the Harvest Fair, 17th of September. A fellow, Bassett, used to bring these boxers down from Swansea—has-beens, like—and we'd get ten bob if we could go three rounds with one of them. Used to get a good hiding, mind, at times, but oh, I loved it. A local fellow, he'd been champion in the Navy, used to put me through my paces, and he used to paste me. Got to get a good hiding to learn, haven't you? I used to hit him, in fear, reaily, to keep him off. "Pull your bloody punches", he'd say, then he'd give me a real belting. But he never marked my face.

Hidings! My mother used to keep a piece of beef hanging up in the pantry, about five or six pounds, two inches thick, and I had to get up on a chair and hold my eye up against that, to take the bruise out. When I was at the Fair, Billy Morgan's wife—he was Champion of Wales—used to look after me. She was very fond of us boys, like, and we used to go to their home. She could give Billy a hiding any day. "Come here, boy", she'd say, and she'd tap my ear and work the blood all out of the bruise.

Anyway, I'm still in one piece, no harm done. Except for my toe-nails. They never recovered. But it didn't stop me dancing. I got to waltz really well, and I learned all the village boys to dance. Two chalk lines, you see, and waltz in between. Oh yes, a bit of a jig in the hall suited me. Half a crown to go in, but often there was a three quid first prize for dancing. I couldn't do it now.

CAPTAIN MOCK

Sea Pilot
Born in Ilfracombe in 1897

Before I went to sea, in 1910, I took a job as an apprentice in a draper's shop, in Swansea. And we used to send parcels down to Gower, with the horse-vans . . . well, to me it was like sending them off to the other side of the Sahara Desert. The end of Gower was so far away. The furthest I had been was Parkmill, on the annual outing . . .

Anyway, during the '39 war we went to live at Porteynon. By

then I was a sea pilot and I took a big interest in the little
schooners, the same ones that used to come over from North
Devon and that, to fetch limestone. I learned that the house we
took over used to be one of the five public houses in Porteynon,
at a time when there would be about twenty-five ships in the
bay on one tide. Well, with at least three men on each ship, I
should think they'd need five pubs, mind they were very small.
Some of the same schooners were still plying between Avon-
mouth and Swansea with grain, and I got to know the old captains and the boats very well. Lovely little things, the small
ketches,—about 60/70 tons they'd be. I used to go to Appledore
quite a bit and mix with the crews and at Bideford I used to see
the old bones of some of these boats, left to rot. Mostly two-
masters they'd be, and the story was, when they were old
they'd go up to Chepstow, say, for loam, and the captains
would anchor in the river, let them settle in the mud over low
water, so that the mud would squeeze over the cracks, then as
the water rose, they'd float off again, and the boats would be
good enough for another couple of months. It saved a visit to dry
dock, you see.

Most of the limestone boats would make for the little coves
in Devon rather than the ports. I remember as a boy, I was born
in Ilfracombe, seeing the rings let into the rocks for mooring the
little boats, along the coast there, and there were, in some
places, mooring posts still in the sand. Heal Bay, near Ilfracombe, they used to visit regularly. The nearer they could get to
the farming areas where the limestone was needed the better
they liked it. They hauled it up the cliff there. Lynmouth too,
and Hartland Quay—though if you look at it, it's difficult to see
how a schooner could sail in there, without any engines. You
see, there's no entrance at all. They'd have to sail in on the
wind, drop sails, then hope for the best.

But the seamen knew their stuff in those days, from the
building of a boat to the handling of it on a tricky coast. I once
heard of a fellow who decided he would build a boat, so he went
down Falmouth way, looked around and found a cove which he
thought would do nicely. So he blocked up the cove, and built
his boat in it, and when she was complete, he let water back

into the cove and floated her. And that boat became a successful trader. These chaps were so well trained they could do all the different stages of the job.

I understand the drill for loading the limestone boats here was to take the stone down by cart from the hill where it was quarried, tip it in a heap on the beach and put a stick to mark the pile. The tide would come in, and when the captain of the little ship came near the stick, he would anchor her, and as the tide went down the men would jump into the water and throw the stones on board. The tide would then float her off, and away she'd go. We hear a lot about the ballast stones they'd bring over from the other side. Well at the same time these stones, mostly greyish-green stones they'd be, would be left where they'd been ejected. Still there, some of them, worn a lot now by the sea, of course. As much as five tons at a time, I reckon. In Swansea, later on, I remember they made good use of these ballast stones. When they were building the piers, they used to give the captains so much for dropping their ballast in such a way as to help with the construction of the jetties, so they killed two birds with one stone!

LILY BUTTON

Schoolmistress
Born at Pitton 1902

"Would you like to take my place?" she said. "Oh, no," I said, "I couldn't do that". But I did, and that's how I came to be a teacher. She was a girl of the village who'd been helping out at the school, and I was just eighteen at the time, living at home, without any particular idea as to what I wanted to do. Never thought of teaching, never had any training for it, of course. "Well", she said, "it's interesting work, and I'm sure you could do it". So I enquired about it;—I never asked anyone to put in a word for me or anything, and I got taken on. That was in

1920, and I was there, teaching the little ones, all my life, for forty-one years, anyway.

I became very fond of the children. There were about forty there then, with two teachers. Things were pretty rough, I remember. Money was very short. The desks were in a terrible state, books and paper were like gold, and I had nothing I could give my little ones that I didn't have to make myself. A lot of drawing with chalk on the walls, with a covering called muraline tacked onto them. I had them all up to seven years of age. Nowadays you'd have a mass of toys, and crayons and jigsaws and things to help you, but I had to spend a lot of my time at home making things, even cutting out numbers to help them learn their figures. You had to handle three different ages and all kinds of ability in the one class. One H.M.I. asked me once ''How on earth do you manage to teach this mixed crowd?'' I used to put them into different divisions for different lessons. I'd set something for one group to do, then I'd take another in reading or written work. The next day it would be the other way round. It seemed to work. The inspector was very impressed anyway.

Once they left my class they moved on to start work for the 11 plus examination. We put everyone in for this except the very backward ones, we didn't concentrate on the brighter ones so that the results would look better. In fact we had very good success in the 11 plus. At one time, I remember, there were eighteen children from the village going to the grammar school at Gowerton. And the standard of intake was high, too. I think it was one of the advantages of a village school. The classes were small. All the children lived around the village. You knew their fathers and their mothers and their grandfathers even from the time they were themselves in school. You knew a lot of their family secrets, too; the children would tell you a lot, but I made a point of never repeating anything I heard that way. Anyway, the atmosphere was always helpful, and one H.M.I. used to bring his colleagues along to visit us. I always used to think: ''Oh, dear, what's wrong now?'' But he'd say: ''I've brought my colleague to see how an ideal village school works''.

To get the best out of a child, I found, you had to show him plenty of love and encouragement. For example, one little boy —I was teaching him to do his numbers. I used to do the numbers with the straight strokes first, like 1, 4, 7 and so on. So I showed him a 7. "Now you try," I said. He brought it to me, "Is that all right?" he said, "Oh," I said, "that's a nice one. Do you know, that's worth a kiss. Now try a few more". He comes back then later and says: "Look at this, miss, don't you think that's worth two kisses?" I wonder if that Gower farmer remembers how he learned his sevens and his success in bargaining! A bit of praise goes a long way, I think.

And don't be unkind in your criticism, that's another thing. I remember one little girl who was usually very good at her work. She'd be about seven. I used to sit by them sometimes and explain or look at their work. One day I said to this girl, "This isn't your book, surely?" . . . it was untidy work, you see "It is, miss", she said. Then there was a pause. "Oh, miss, give it to me, I want to do it all out again. I'll never do untidy work again, I promise". She knew in a minute, you see, without my having to spell it all out to her.

A number of pupils came back to me to thank me for teaching them the tables. They're very valuable, I think, but not fashionable perhaps. Oh, I believed in the tables. And another thing, since we were in the country I thought they ought to know the wild flowers. So as the flowers opened, they used to bring one to school, and the one who had brought it had to enter it on a long run of paper I kept beside the board. They regarded this as a great honour, and it was surprising what they learned.

In my early days some parents used to keep the children home to help on the farm, especially at hay and potato harvests. But that habit grew less, there seemed to be a general desire in the village to get as much out of schooling as they could. Discipline was never a problem either, we had no cane, and the worst punishment we could inflict was keeping someone in during break, doing extra work. This meant they couldn't play 'cat and dog' on the hill or rounders near Watts Pool. They didn't like missing that. No, the only thing approaching any kind of trouble was when we had evacuees staying with us during the last war. A lot of the newcomers were not up to the standard of the school. The parents of the evacuee children said this themselves. But we had some problem children then, I can tell you. I remember one little boy of six, he was such a nice little chap, but he was obsessed with money. He was always rattling coins, and I told him not to bring money to school, "You might lose it", I'd say, "or someone might take it". But next day it was the same, so I kept a sharp eye on him, and I found that during the day he had got his hand in every child's pocket. I asked to see the money he had, and "Would you like some, miss?", he asked with a winning smile. They found later that he used to go into people's houses on the way home from school, and they had to put him in reins to keep him under control. He didn't want to learn much, but he was ever such a nice little boy.

Most of the evacuees fitted in well eventually, and picked up quite a bit. Some stayed on here for four years, and they still come back to the village now and again, bringing their own children with them. Lots of my old pupils come back, in fact, and call in to see me. Usually I've no idea who they are. Only the other day, we'd just come home from town, and there was a big car standing outside our gate. I thought at first it was a family about to have a picnic. They don't mind where they stop sometimes. But then a gentleman came up the path . . . "I've been searching for you," he said to me, "You know who I am, don't you?" But the last time I'd seen him he was a little boy in school. He was the son of a coastguard who was stationed here at the time. "I've been all round the village looking for you. My mother will be pleased when I tell her I've been to see my teacher. I've got my two boys outside, I'd like them to meet you . . ." Odd, isn't it?

But I was of course a fixture, in the same place for a long time. As someone said, I'd become part of the scenery. One day I was explaining to a class about an old building near here, and I said to them . . . "Well, it's quite close to where I live, you know where I live, don't you?" "Yes, miss," someone said, "in the school".

It was a very sad time for me when I retired. For a long time I couldn't bring myself to go past the school building. Perhaps it was a kind of envy, but I hated the idea of anyone else being there, in my place. Of course the school itself has gone now, no more real village school. It's nice to see children from all parts enjoying the building as an outdoor activities centre. But it's not the same, is it?

I did become very attached to my children. They would often call me "Mammy", and then get all confused. Another inspector said once: "You're for all the world like a family here, and they're all so fair-haired, you could easily be their mother" . . . And that's how it's been, I suppose . . .

ELIZABETH DAVIES

District Nurse and Baker's Wife
Born at Pencoed 1905

I came down to Gower on July the first, 1930, to Reynoldston. From near Bridgend I was, my mother was Welsh. I remember it was a beautiful day when we arrived. The conductor stopped the bus outside the pub, the King Arthur, and pointed across to the nurses' cottage, I can see him now. The housekeeper was standing at the gate as we came along, and she called out to us: "Would you like a boiled egg?" There were two of us, and we had to pay her 10/- a week and feed her. She was a bit too fond of her glass of stout, but she was alright.

In those days of course we were paid by the Nursing Association, and people used to pay for our services, 15/- for a confinement, say. We got three pounds a week, and we were on call for twenty-four hours. We had a phone on the wall, but people preferred to come and fetch us. Oil lamps, W.C. out the back, and we had to carry every drop of water from near the Post Office. The paper on the wall had been there for donkey's years, and when we asked to have it redone—I came from a spotlessly clean home myself—they weren't willing, so we set to and did it all out ourselves. They wouldn't do anything for us there.

The housekeeper used to sleep in an old chair bed in the kitchen.

People didn't run to the doctor in those days, of course. Because they had to pay, and you know what Gower people are like! Anyway there wasn't a lot of money around. No real poverty, but it was touch and go, and if they were poor they wouldn't show it. Living conditions were really primitive. But usually very clean. Some houses I went to were white-washed right through, every room in the house. I was a bit on the friendly side myself, and people were very kind. We had to do every sort of thing. One of the first cases I had was a woman with her face half-eaten away with cancer, and there were old men with cancer of the rectum, hopeless cases. People would have to supply their own dressings, and they'd manage to boil up some water for us, but that was all. And they were pretty stingy with the cotton wool. No one went to hospital in those days, of course.

We had to get around to places on push-bike. But usually I found I could walk as quick. The nurse with me rode over to Llanrhidian once, I walked there across the Bryn and got there first. The roads were terrible. Mr Williams of Rhossili Post Office was a wonderful help, he was the first to have a car, and he had a motor-bike. All hours of the night, he was ready to help us and the people of the village.

There were two doctors in these parts then, both pretty old, and not very good friends, really. Very jealous of each other, it seems. I don't know that they ever spoke to each other. Funny thing, because as doctors they were marvellous men. There was Dr Moreton, and Dr Baker Jones, who was older, very gruff, but he was a man, he'd tackle anything. He'd look after you. I remember we'd been on a case in Cheriton all day long, operation, no anaesthetics then of course, you had to go through it all. Eleven o'clock at night when we came away. Then he said to me: "We can't go home yet, you know, oh no, we've got to call at Lunnon". There was a man dying of T.B. We got there by midnight! Imagine asking anyone to do today what we had to do. I remember Dr Moreton coming to me one evening, and he said: "I want one of you to go to Green Cwm, that's out among

Rushbrook Cottage, the Nurses' Cottage, *ca.* 1906

the woods beyond Parkmill''. The gamekeeper was ill, he was only 33, a fine looking chap, but he had T.B. And his cottage was in the middle of the woods. ''He's had a bad haemorrhage, one of you will have to stay the night . . . if you don't go, I'll have to''. ''Poor dab,'' I thought, I couldn't see the old man going all that way. I was only in my twenties, after all. So I set out. I was terrified by the time I got to Parkmill, so I knocked on the door of the miller's house, I can see him now. He'd just finished his work and had his coarse apron on, but he took a long stick and led me right to the cottage. Anyway, I went in, the gamekeeper was lying on a sofa under the window, and his wife was there. There were lace curtains on the windows, and, you see, brought up in a town, like, I had a thing about curtains. I always draw them at night, and hate anyone peeping in. But she didn't draw them, you see, and I was sitting in a chair near the window, and I was terrified in case some face would appear at the window. What with the hooting of the owls and all that, I was dead scared. All night. In the morning he said to me: ''I was watching you nurse, you never took you eyes off me all night''. Well, I thought, one eye perhaps, but I had the other on that window. The poor boy died soon after. T.B. was common in those days, but there was a terrible lot of cancer too.

Some people were funny. One old man had bad legs, and I used to go up every day to dress his varicose ulcers. He used to kill pigs, and up over the grate in the charnel he had loads of ham and bacon covered with newspaper. He used to try to get me to come on Sundays . . . ''I'll keep you in bacon, if you come up here on Sundays''. Sorry, I had to say, not allowed except in an emergency. But he kept on. No use.

Then there was old Mrs Bevan, living opposite him. I used to call and bath her. But she used to get up first thing and wash the kitchen floor and clean up everything, then go back to bed if you please and wait for me to come to give her a bath. Nice old thing she was, but we had to put a stop to that.

One of the nurses had her own remedy which she used to deal out . . . linseed oil and white lime. We used to take it around with us, wonderful for burns it was. And goose-grease, that was a winner.

There was a funny side, mind,—I suppose you have to laugh sometimes to stop yourself crying. One young man was dying of cancer, and he couldn't pass his urine. I was with the doctor, holding the jug while he used the catheter, and the poor man was saying: "Am I peeing, doctor?" "Yes, my man, you are peeing", said Doctor Jones. I could have wept really, but it was so comical, this old man doing all he could for the young one. But he died all the same.

Occasionally we got a tip, and Lady Blytheswood would send us a couple of pheasants for Christmas. But once a tip went the wrong way. I used to go to an old woman at Rose Cottage. Every morning like clockwork, she used to do everything in bed, you know. Then she'd paint her face with it. And I had to clean her up. One day Dr Jones came along while I was there. "Well, well, well", he said, "I didn't realise you had to do anything like this". And fair play, he went and told the man in the village who looked after her affairs what I'd had to do. You'll never believe it, but he gave twenty pounds—not to me, to the Nursing Association!

Oh, yes, people suffered then, they had hard lives, and they accepted this. Today people cry more easily, they're softer, they get everything so easy. Terrible lot of money wasted under the National Health, I think. Too many people get more than they want, and they don't appreciate it. I don't think that's good.

GLYN RICHARDS

Rocket apparatus crewman
Born in Rhossili 1909

People often wonder what there was to do in the village years ago. I can tell them. Plenty. When I was a boy living in Rhossili the main things were: in the winter there was draughts and whist and in the summer quoits, and football,—no cricket. The quoits was a great thing. We had a quoits league, each village

had a team of eight and we used to play every Saturday afternoon. First of all you needed 2 clay beds; you dug out a patch
about four foot square and filled it with clay. The bed was raised
up, to face you, like, and there'd be a peg in the middle. The
beds would be 21 yards from each other, and a pair from each
village, with two quoits each would play against a pair from
another village. Nearest the peg of course would be the one to
score. Up to twenty-one. The quoits would be nearly four
pounds each, and, oh yes, they'd be well looked after. We'd polish them until you could see your face in them. By gosh, we
wouldn't let them rust! At the end of the summer they'd be
washed and greased and put by till the next season. Very keen
we were. There were different types of players with the quoit.
You'd get one who could throw a very flat quoit and this would
come down flop, you see, and if he happened to be around the
peg, you'd never get near him. Another would pitch it up on its
side. Unless the others were very close, this could pitch right on
the peg. He'd cut you out in a minute, but the old stager with a
flat quoit, he wouldn't give you a chance, you could bound off
or slide over him. Oh yes, we had a very good team indeed, in
Rhossili. I could just about hold my own, nothing outstanding.

When it came then to draughts, it was mostly the same little
crowd of fellows, and they were good at this, too. Real wizards
some of them were, excellent.

Then there'd be the whist drives, in the evenings in the village hall. Married v single. My gosh, we had some really good
nights at that. These married couples, you see. Of course, we
single chaps had our choice. There was always a squabble as to
who should play with Annie Gibbs. Annie was a character at
whist, and she was single. More often than not I played with
her. And she had the luck of the devil at cards, it was quite un-
canny. She's gone some years now, of course, but even now if
you play the ace, king, queen, someone will say "Boy, you've
got an Annie Gibbs hand tonight". It still lives today. By gosh,
she could trot 'em out. She was stone deaf too, and it wasn't
surprising that she had the reputation of being, well, you know,
a bit of a witch. If anything went wrong in the village, she'd

often get blamed for it. And her luck at cards seemed always a bit suspicious, like.

Another bit of fun we had in the village, round Christmastime, was the Horse's Head. When I was about twenty a few of us decided to revive the old custom of the Mari Lwyd, which was just dying out. I remember now going to look for this horse's head. We knew a horse had been buried in a field at Kimley Moor, years and years before. So we went and dug it up and sure enough, the head was as good as new, the real thing. So we took it over to a fellow by the name of Willie Clement of Porteynon, who was a dab hand at dressing up a horse's head. He used to get the proper stuff, you know, ribbons and all that, and it was a sight to behold what he could make out of it. Then at Christmas, we used to go around with this old thing, the fellow underneath the sheet—usually me—would work the jaw with a piece of wire, very realistic. We'd go to a house, and p'rhaps they'd be having supper, so the old horse would go to the table

Mari Lwyd at Mumbles.

and catch hold of a piece of cake or something in his jaws and champ away as we went off. Or he'd snap his jaws and try to scare the girls, we really did have fun out of that.

Horse's Head Song

Once I was a young horse
And in my stable gay
I had the best of everything
Of barley oats and hay,
But now I am an old horse
My courage is getting small
I'm 'bliged to eat the sour grass
That grows beneath the wall.

Chorus:
  Poor old horse, let him die,
  Poor old horse, let him die.

I've eaten all my oats and hay
Devoured all my straw,
I can hardly move about
Nor can my carriage draw:
With these poor weary limbs of mine
I've travelled many miles
Over hedges, bramble bushes,
Gates and narrow stiles.

Chorus:
  Poor old horse, let him die,
  Poor old horse, let him die.

People used to give us money, for charity. Some of them would give us a bribe not to come into the house. By gosh they were times, I can tell you . . .

One thing we boys were expected to help in was the rocket crew. The idea of this was to get the people off a ship in trouble close to the shore, when the lifeboat—from Mumbles or Tenby couldn't. Same bunch of fellows again would volunteer for it. The full complement was eighteen. Every two months or so we turned out for a practice. There was a rocket post on the cliff, above Rhossili Bay, still there, of course, and from just below the station we'd fire the rocket out towards it, with a fine line attached to it. Three or four men would follow the line and make it fast on the post, which was the ship. The line had a hawser attached to it, so this would then be hauled out by the men at the post, and at the end of the hawser would be the breeches buoy, a sort of life-jacket in the form of a large pair of trouser legs which would hold a person securely, while one lot would pull on a so-called whip to haul the breeches-buoy out and another lot would pull on another whip to haul it ashore. Then it was all made fast at the shore end with the big anchor. Each of the rocket crew had a specific job to do. We all had numbers, I was number ten and my job was to assist number one, who was responsible for the rocket. Four horses were needed to drag the cart and all the gear to wherever a ship was in trouble. At least, they would take it as far as they could, then you'd have to manhandle the gear . . .

One wreck I particularly remember was that of the *Roche Castle* in 1937 near Paviland cliffs. We first had a message to say

'Roche Castle'.

there was a boat ashore somewhere between Mumbles and Rhossili, pretty vague. Then they were able to tell us it was between Oxwich Point and Rhossili. I had moved to Horton by then, so two of us started from that way towards Rhossili about 11 o'clock, and we were the first to spot the boat. It was a devilishly rough night, and the fog was very dense. But there she was, quite close in. The tide was out and she didn't seem to be stuck fast, but settling on the rocks, which are murderous about there. Anyway, it was getting rougher all the time. The rocket crew arrived, and the fellow in charge called out to the boat and told the men to walk ashore, which they could have done easily. No trouble at all. But they said no, they decided to stay, thinking she'd float when the tide came up. But she did the exact opposite of course. The moment the tide started to come in, the waves caught her up and instead of floating her free, they brought her in further, and soon the men on board were in a panic. We had by then set everything up, just in case. So now they couldn't wait to be saved.

The difficulty we had then was that the boat started to sway all over the place with the rough sea as it came in. Instead of coming off one at a time, the first two of the crew decided to put one leg each in the breeches buoy, and hold on to each other. Well, I can see it now. Just as we were about to haul them in, and they left the top of the ship, one great wave came and carried the boat forward slackening the cable. Of course the next thing the breeches buoy was in the water, and the fellows were being dragged across the rocks. Then back it swung again, and became a sort of catapult. You never saw anything like it in your life. One of the men fell out of the breeches, into the sea, and that was the end of him. The other one managed to cling on till he was near the edge of the surf, and we managed to haul him out just in time. After that, we waited a little longer until she was really fast, then we fixed the anchor again, and we brought the rest of the crew in without much trouble. We saved eleven, but lost one and for that particular rescue the team had a special award for the best rescue service of the year in Britain, the first time it had come to Wales. We didn't feel we were heroes or anything, we just took the rocket crew duty for granted, it was an honour really to belong to it. And we hardly did it for the money. We'd get a couple of quid for turning out and five bob for a practice! We just felt we were doing our duty for the village, as a team, and we enjoyed it.

Most of my working life I've been concerned with water supply to the villages. It began during the Second World War, and I suppose it was the biggest boon that came to these parts. Though you wouldn't have thought so at first. It was a funny thing, the water that was being piped was the same water that people had been getting from the well, no different at all, but there was an almighty uproar about it, it was now far too hard, they said, and what could be done about it? Same water, exactly. But now it was furring up the kettles and that; terrible to-do. Send for the Ministry of Health man to sort it out! And indeed, he did come down, he took samples, and his findings were, that of all the supplies he had tested, this was the nearest to pure water you could get. "Now you take Swansea water", he said, "the softest water you could find anywhere. But the tooth decay is the highest in Britain. Now here you've got the very best water, full of calcium, and you want to destroy it". It wasn't softened. I mean, they hadn't made any objections till it was in the pipes, isn't it typical?

The first mains, at Rhossili, were lengthened then to supply Porteynon and Horton, which seemed a bit much. But then they decided to stretch it further, to Oxwich, then even to Reynoldston, but that broke the camel's back. They got into trouble. There were shortages in the summer, cuts in water overnight—which was useless in my opinion, because if you know the water's going to be turned off say at seven in the evening, you make sure the bath is full, and all the pots and pans you can find, then what happens? At seven in the morning you've probably still got your bath full, so up with the plug, and away it goes. More waste than if it had been left alone. In Reynoldston itself they sometimes had to get the fire engines to pump the mains full from a well just below the post office. The next big step was the pumping station at Parkmill, and there they drew upon water from Swansea . . .

Since then you can definitely taste the water, it is chlorinated fairly heavily. Though you get more effect of this if you're at the end of a main. The asbestos pipes seemed to taint the water if it was left standing in the mains. Every so often, at points nearest the sea, we used to open the hydrants and let the water flow out for about ten minutes, so that the mains were well flushed.

There are a wonderful lot of springs in Gower, the lack is not of water but of storage. And some of these old springs used to be quite famous. Take the one at Talgarth's Well. That never freezes up, must come from a great depth, and never changes temperature throughout the year. A lot of people used to go to that well for water, they used to say it was beautifully-tasting water, wouldn't drink any other. In fact, even after the mains were laid, some still used to go and get a canful of Talgarth water for drinking. Then there was the Iley water near the old parsonage in Rhossili Bay. By gosh, that was cold water. It was a favourite of a lot of people. There was a sheep wash on the stream too, but it was so icy they would fill up the old pound today, like, and leave it stand for a few days to warm up a bit in the sun. It was very, very cold, and as clear as crystal. It was very noted. Rhossili water, from the hill above the church, wasn't rated so high. Nobody liked that much for some reason.

KENNETH HARDCASTLE

Coastguard
Came to Rhossili January 1976

I've been a coastguard now for three and a half years, that's all. But I'm sorry I didn't get in a long time ago, its a great life. For twenty years I was in the Royal Navy and the Merchant Navy, and then I worked on the docks in Liverpool. But that was an in-secure job if you like, you had to save up for going on strike all the time, always watching the pennies. So, it was my brother's idea, to apply for the coastguard service, I'd never have thought of it. But it's a good job, this, a worthwhile job. Very different of course from the early days. In a place like this all you'd have then was one man with a telescope, and maybe a phone. Now the whole set-up is more sophisticated, with radio, and inter-comm. and that, most of your information comes by radio. It's not so much what you can see now but what you can hear. We've got a look-out on the cliff edge, but that's not much help now, except to deal with a casualty. I mean, it takes fifteen minutes to get back to the office here, and that's running.

We rely a lot now on auxiliaries—people with boats who are auxiliary coastguards and they have radio, so we use them a lot. If there are half a dozen boats in the bay, say, and one of them is an auxiliary, we can rely on that lot being covered. You see, we work in a fairly local area these days. The shipping lanes are five or six miles away now, and the larger ships can get their own gale warnings on the radio. We put up gale cones at the look-out, and I have to set a bad weather watch day and night when the wind is Force 6, for that I can call out land auxiliaries, and in an emergency, there's the rocket crew.

What I like about working in a place like this is the freedom of movement you're allowed, nobody sitting on your back all the time. I was in a bigger station to begin with, but this is a different life altogether. If you go out on patrol here it's up to you, to be honest with yourself and your superiors. And you get more job-satisfaction. If you help somebody it's a good feeling to know that you've done something for somebody. You don't want the glory, it's just knowing, that's enough.

The one big drawback is that you don't know when you're going to be free, off duty. At Mumbles, say, with the watch-keeping, six hours on, and two days off every so often, you can at least write it down: I'll be off this time next week. But here you can be called out at any moment. That's how it happens. In the summer-time especially. There are a lot of people about these days who don't know too much about the sea. Some of these new boat-owners, for example, from the Midlands, say. It's amusing sometimes. We had one chap, come down the Bristol Channel, making his way to Aberystwyth. And the only charts he had on board were road maps of South Wales! He ended up in the Burry Estuary, took a wrong turning. He had to put his boat on a trailer, and go to Aberystwyth by road after all.

You can't hope to catch all these stupid 'sailors'; you see, what a lot of them do is this: they take their new boat down to the water, then after a few weeks, back it goes to Birmingham, and gets laid up for nearly twelve months. By which time it can dry up, the seams tend to open out, so that when they put it in the water again, next thing they're in trouble, crying out for a pump. That's more and more of a problem to us.

Another bane of our lives is air-beds. They can be so dangerous with an off-shore wind. You can't hope to stop them all. So we just walk along a beach and if we see anything inflatable we just try to warn them to be careful. "But the tide's coming in," they say. They don't realise that airbeds and things like that are not affected by the tide at all, only by the wind. We've had numbers of kids carried out. Often saved by a helpful boat in the bay. Or the rescue boat from Horton or Burry Port. It makes me mad sometimes because people won't take to be told. But you have to be tactful at all times, the image you try to put to the public is one of being helpful. Because in the end you rely on their help and co-operation, for information, say. Often it's misleading, mind, and cock-eyed, but you have to keep being diplomatic. You know some fellow's a flaming idiot but all you can say is "Yes, sir, you're quite right." Your private thoughts are one thing, but you try not to speak them out. I had a good example of that sort of public help a few weeks ago. A man phoned up to say he had come across a round black object on a North Gower beach. With a hole in the middle. Looked dangerous he said. "Don't try to move it, sir", I said, "I'll be there right away". "No fear, I'll not damn well go near it", he said. Anyway, I went across, found the black object, it was the wheel off a toy tractor. I showed it to some boys in the village. "Do you know what this is?" "It's the wheel off a toy tractor" they all said, without hesitation. It defies imagination, doesn't it? This nut case thinking it was a mine, and dragging me over . . . never mind, that's what we try to teach the public . . . "any unfamiliar object . . ." and all that.

Worms Head is a constant problem with us. We have a board now where we put up the times when it is safe to cross the causeway. Because if they get stuck out there, they're there for seven hours. You can have five hours or so out there between tides, but quite a few people can't tell the time or something, and get caught. Unless it's cold and misty we don't bother any more, or if we know there are no children or babies with the party, we just leave them until the causeway is open again, or if it's dark, assist them across with a searchlight. If there's an accident, and I need a helicopter, I can get one, cost doesn't come into it. It's a bit of a danger, the Worm, but I think that's what attracts people to it. It's a marvellous spot, of course. If you are out there on your own, right at the end of the Head, nothing else but you and the sea and the birds, it's quite an experience.

I thought hang-gliding was going to be a bit of a menace at first, when it started, they seemed to be crashing all over the place, arms, legs and collar-bones got broken, but they're more expert now. Even now they've got to be watched, but their rules say they can only fly the ridge and the cliffs and they can only land on the beach or back on the hill. But if someone can't help landing in a field, you can't argue the point with him, can you, especially if he's carted off to hospital. And it's interesting, it's doing quite a lot of good for the village, too, attracting sight-seers, I mean.

We don't have to cover the coast on foot as they used to. We go everywhere by Landrover now. Well, almost everywhere. I'm thinking of one day early this summer. It was dusk, late evening, and we had a casualty—a lost child over at Broughton Sands. I found crowds of people searching for this kid, without any trace. They were beginning to talk about helicopters. Anyway, the kid was found eventually, not lost at all, she had been looked after in a caravan site nearby. I took her grandfather with me to pick her up, and there was an auxiliary coastguard and a lot of gear besides. On the way back we met the rest of her family, her mother, her grandmother, her brother, her father, I took them all aboard, so I had a packed Landrover, with a top weight of gear. I'll take them back to where they're staying, I thought, and that'll be my good deed for today. So we set out on a way over sand-dunes—but taking one nasty slope, the vehicle that can go anywhere and do anything, refused, and very slowly it turned over on its side, in the pitch black. No one was hurt, but they were all more frightened than they'd been all day. So much for my Good Samaritan act!

I don't get told about much contraband being washed up these days. The coastguard never did, of course, but I believe people are getting more honest, not so short of money perhaps. But there's still a surprising amount of wood. Not so surprising really, because I remember when I was on cargo boats, the first job we had to do when the boat set out for sea after being in dock was to clear the decks and give them a good wash down, and there was inevitably a lot of timber left lying and not stored away, from repairs and such work, so over it went—into the biggest dust bin in the world. That's where most of your timber comes from. Gosh, I wish I could now lay my hands on some of the stuff I threw overboard. Out in the Channel there, there's floating masses of timber, a southerly wind brings some of it ashore here, a northerly wind takes it onto North Devon beaches. Then out it goes again, up and down with the wind and the tides.

I mentioned the rocket crew. Well, you know who they are, they're an old established bunch of volunteers who bring out the means of saving lives by sending a line out to a ship in trouble near the cliffs and bringing the crew off by breeches buoy, a sort of trousers a man gets into to be hauled to safety over the waves. If there's an incident where I decide they can help, I send up a maroon, from a trench in my garden here. In theory this brings the company to the station at the double. But many people can't hear it because of the wind, so I call them by telephone as well. I must say we always get a marvellous response, never any trouble to drop whatever they're doing and turn out. Of course not a lot of vessels run aground these days. But the men are very useful if we have to make a search for something, or somebody. And that happens often enough. There was a sad case only a few weeks ago. A boy, he'd been fishing, rough sea, too close to the water's edge, was caught by a wave and disappeared from the ledge he was on. It seemed hard to believe, but we could find no trace of him at all, and he never was found. A very odd thing, though. Two days later I found two pullovers of his, on the very ledge he went from, he probably had managed to take them off, I think. I've thought a lot about that since, and I feel sure now that though we couldn't see him during our search, he could in some way see us. We've had some distressing accidents—and suicides—on these cliffs. Too often it's a case of parents not being vigilant about their children.

A lot of our work is complementary to that of other organisations. The police, of course, mostly. Then it might be the National Trust, or the R.S.P.C.A., or the conservationists or the Life Savers or the Naturalists' Trust. We've got no authority, but we go as far as we can. People, especially children, come and tell us they've seen a seal stranded, in some inaccessible place, or bring us a wounded sea-bird, or a lost dog. The other day,—we had a good laugh over this . . . someone brought in a seagull, found him on the beach, apparently helpless for some reason. Anyway, he turned out to be quite tame, we gave him bread and milk and stuff, and he'd let you stroke him even, really tame, couldn't find anything wrong with him. He was here a couple of days, then he flew off, seemed to be quite O.K. Then blow me, a couple of days later someone brought another seagull to us, found in the same way, but it was the same gull—definitely the same one, I recognised him! He got the same treatment, then off he flew. And the same thing happened, true, two or three times after that. Talk about a fly bird! These are the nicer sides of the job.

As I say, in this job you're free, and you're not free. If you go for a walk, an ordinary walk, on a beautiful day, on a fine bit of cliff-top, you can't get away from it, the fact that you're still on duty, you're committed, it's a matter of conscience. But where else would you get a place to live like this—and be paid for doing it?

JACK TANNER

Ploughman
Born at Pilton Green 1917

My grandfather was the last practising weaver in Gower. He
had his water mill at Cheriton, and when he died, in 1932, the
loom was still working, turning out blankets, and cloth of all
kinds, especially for suits. For years he used to walk into
Swansea, carrying four pairs of hefty blankets, over half a
hundredweight of a pack, and take a train to Neath. He'd sell
the blankets at Neath Fair, then walk all the way home again.
He used to do this regularly. He used to be a great man with the
scythe, too, so he used to take on jobs of cutting the corn on
farms. He had nine children, after all, and he needed all the
extra he could get. They'd go out, he and my father, at day-
break, four o'clock in the morning, and cut four acres of barley,
say, and by the time a boy brought out a jar of beer and their
breakfast, at 9 o'clock, they'd be all finished, and resting under
a hedge, the four acres had been scythed. Just think of it today!
   My father came to work on a farm in South Gower, he was
only earning 10/- a week, so he took a job as horseman at
Weavers' flour mills in Swansea, twenty-six shillings a week.
Good money, but within five years he had to come out with
flour dust on his lungs. At the time I was born he was back here,
catching rabbits for a living. In his first winter he snared over
two thousand rabbits! We used to be over-run with rabbits
once, and when later we started market-gardening, and we
began growing a few cabbage and carrots, gor, they were a
menace. We had to put wire fencing around everything, and
sink it a foot down into the ground; if we didn't, the cabbage
and carrots would disappear and every swede would be marked.
Everything stank of rabbits. Cattle and sheep wouldn't graze
within twenty feet of the hedges the grass was so foul. I'll say
this, myxomatosis was a Godsend to us, best thing that ever
happened. It was a terrible thing, a very ugly sight, but I was
mighty glad to see the rabbits go, I can tell you. And within a
year you know my lambs got so fat I couldn't sell them, and in

three years I increased my breeding flock from 50 to 150 ewes on the same acreage. The direct result of wiping out the rabbits. No more snaring then, of course. No one would eat a rabbit any more!

With pheasants it was different. It was a dangerous game but worth it, so I thought at one time. That was when I left the secondary school. My father had been took ill and I came out at fifteen. Which may have been just as well, because the war was on, and sixteen of my class-mates ended up on the Roll of Honour. I could have been the seventeenth. Anyway, my trouble then was that I had no wages, so the temptation was too strong, like. Our fields were close up to the Penrice Woods, the pheasants came so thick and heavy down onto our fields, and they were making four shillings a pair,—so over the years I kept a shop in Sketty well supplied, they used to phone down with a code message for me about how many 'ducks' they needed, and all that. It was my cigarette and beer money, anyway. I suppose I must have knocked off over three hundred before they caught me in the woods one November night with a gun. My worry then was, of course, if you were caught shooting pheasants, you had no hope of being given a farm, or of getting one after your father. And it so happened that my father died in the December, just a month after I had been caught. Of course, the first thing I did was to apply to take over the tenancy from the following March. As luck had it, the War Executive Committee stepped in and pointed out that I had been classed as a Grade A farmer, so they had no option but to give it to me. A year or two earlier, mind, and I'd have been sent packing. But the pheasants were a menace, too, they'd come in their hundreds when you were sowing and pick up the corn from the drills as you went. I remember my uncle once told me: "Sow one grain to rot, one to grow, one for the pigeon and one for the crow". Well we had to put one out for the pheasant, too. Still, they were good old times.

My main interest in life though has been ploughing. I started off as a youngster, ploughing with horses. I was about sixteen when a fellow happened to see me ploughing a little field of two and half acres, one Sunday morning. "Why don't you come

along to a ploughing match?'' he said, ''you've got nothing to be afraid of.'' So I had a look at what Jim Harry was doing, and I thought to myself, ''You're doing a damn sight better than that, boy.'' So that started me off. I entered for the next ploughing match, at Penmaen. My father wasn't willing at first, ''You can't enter with that harness, boy, 'tisn't good enough.'' Pride in the turn-out was a big thing. I know he couldn't afford it, but on the Monday he went into town. And back he came with a new pair of collars, bridles, chains and the rest and he set me up to go onto that field. He got up at four in the morning to plait the tails and the manes of the two horses and polished and shone up the brasses. They used to plait the tail in three pieces, then turn it up into a bow with red white and blue ribbons, then the mane the same, bows all the way down. It was a wonderful sight, mind, and I can tell you I felt very proud when I drove onto that field with my pair in full turn-out. I came third that first time, but it wasn't long before I won the champion class seven times in a row.

I always preferred ploughing with horses. I could sing to them. A neighbour of ours used to say he had enjoyed the operatic session I'd been giving, singing on top of my voice, marvellous, all day long. But after we had a tractor I never sang again. Many people think there's nothing to ploughing a field, but it shows they know nothing about it. The aim of all ploughing is the same, of course: whatever trash is on the top of the soil has got to be completely buried, so that it'll make humus for the following year, and so that nothing grows through. I could take you to the farms around here with good ploughmen, and they are the ones that need to spend less on weed-killer than anyone else. Ploughing straight is the most efficient way of doing this. So if you haven't got the eye, you can forget about it. On the other hand if you can do it, it's as easy as going to bed. Any fool can do it with a tractor. But to drive two horses dead straight across a field is a gift. Of course with horses you are looking at the work in front of you, whereas with a tractor you have to look back at it all the time. It makes quite a difference to the finish. You are allowed two red and white markers in a competition, set out on the field and you have to keep those in line. If you can see them both, you've got a crook. It's funny, the appeal of the straight furrow. Our local match—we used to have two in Gower, with about thirty competitors, all finished now—would be held on a Thursday. On the following Sunday morning, you could go to that field, and there'd be a crowd there, keen old boys even walking with two sticks, and all the local experts would be there, walking that field, about fifty or sixty of them, all contradicting the judges, but they'd all stop and admire a dead straight furrow. The judges themselves would be the same. If your line wasn't straight, they'd just pass you by. Oh yes, I used to enjoy the Sunday morning turn-out as much as the day itself.

It wasn't long before I took an interest in the executive side of ploughing matches. I became a site director, first for the Welsh, then eventually the British Ploughing Association meeting. Then in 1970 I got the chance of being a joint director of the World match, at Taunton. In the end I had to plan the 200 acres on my own. I didn't sleep for three or four nights before that, I can tell you. But as a result I was awarded a gold medal for an "outstanding contribution to the World Ploughing Match". I've been all over the world since then, with ploughing, and in 1973 I was picked as team manager to the British team to go to America. I had a wonderful trip out there, all paid for. And I had a chance of correcting the impression of the Yanks that I'd got during the war. The ones I met then belonged to an Advance Landing Unit, that took over a site near us and used the nearby beaches for landing exercises. It so happened that my farm was inside the perimeter of the camp, so to fetch the cows in the morning I had to pass ten separate guards and show my pass. And from the ten I'd be lucky to get three "Good mornings". They had no time for us, everything they did was pretty high-handed. They charged around with bulldozers to make roads for their DKWs and tore down hedges; one of them went through six fields of mine and smashed every gate. Perhaps they thought they had more serious work to do than to consider us. In a way they did, because on the Sunday before D-day they left here, about 20,000 of them, and I heard they were first in on the

Ploughing Match at Parc le Breos, 1950.

beaches a few days later and took the brunt of the Normandy attack. Most of them were wiped out, so I heard.

In America in '73 I met mostly families with an agricultural background, a completely different class of Yank altogether, I'm glad to say.

Of course, the Scandinavians are the boys who dominate the World championships these days. There are about twenty countries represented with two competitors from each, mostly Europe, Africa and the Americas, but even Japan is interested now. There have been big improvements in the last ten years in the plough itself, the work the modern plough will do is really fantastic. And the world champion of a few years ago wouldn't stand a chance today against say, the Norwegians, who won this year. You see, in this country we plough on an average six inches deep, so our ploughs were always made to turn a six by nine furrow. If you want to cut 7 inches down, you've got to go to 11 inches wide, or 8 inches by 12. Holland for example wouldn't dream of ploughing less than 8 inches, in their soft polder stuff. Now the new Norwegian plough can handle any depth of soil, provided it is solid. The Ransome, now, that could handle a very light soil and it used to be the plough for Britain, even with horses.

As equipment improved, the standard of ploughing in Gower got steadily better, I think, but since the local ploughing matches were abandoned, it's certainly gone down hill. Pity. Not that there is a lack of talent. I'm coaching one boy now, he's a budding champion if ever I saw one, he certainly has a real future in front of him, in the Welsh if not the British championships. It's a fascinating game, mind.

RON PARRY

Entertainer
Born in Llanrhidian 1922

As a boy I was never keen on farming, but here I am now, back at it, helping my brother, and dreadfully happy, I must say. Being a bachelor, you see, I'm obliged to live somewhere where I get good keep, and that I do get from my sister-in-law, fair play. But I grew up on my father's farm, in the thirties, and it was so hard, there was a vicious slump about, and prices cracked, rotten cheap they got, and it put farmers in a very queer shape. Mind, the Penrice estate was very kind to my father and he got on great with them, he was a good tenant, always prepared to do his own repairs. Once we were putting back pantiles on a roof after a storm, Bridgwater pantiles, baked clay, fantastic things, but they were not fastened down, and they could blow off sometimes. And the agent came along and said: "My word, you're doing a damn good job there, very nice, we haven't got many like you, who take the trouble to do their own repairs." But my Dad was very keen, and Penrice used to be helpful with the rent and things, on Lady Day and Michaelmas, big words in those days, eh? And her Ladyship used to pass by frequently, I used to wave to her, and the surveyor would turn up in a smart little pony and trap, even drive over the ploughed fields to see the farmer, who didn't like this. But there was great feeling between my Dad and the estate, and that was very nice, because he lived to see himself the owner of his farm, after her Ladyship passed on.

I went away from the farm then, and tried engineering, for four years, and though I decided there was nothing in it for me I really am a born mechanic and now I'm back with my brother I do all the maintenance work except welding. I can do engines of all kinds, clutches, gear boxes, back-axles, the lot. I must say I was glad to see the tractor coming to the farm. I didn't care much for horses, but it was great fun, sitting on a tractor. Though the diesels are much noisier than the old Fordsons used to be. Livestock on the other hand now, there's a lot of worry

with them. Lambing is a round-the-clock job. Pigs the same.
And animals have a knack of dying, or falling sick. The other
day we had a sow, with ten lovely piglets, her first litter, I only
turned my back for a moment, and snap snap, she bit every one
of them just here, behind the shoulder, and they all died.
Pierced their lungs. One bite's enough, not hard. Anyway, ten
went like that. Her sister reared nine, no trouble. Animals are
pleasant little things . . . but I prefer to potter, use my hands.
I've got an old Austin, 1959, and I keep it nice. No, the finest
tools you could have are the ones you were born with. The
hands are clever, I think, don't you? Great tools. Something
that animals haven't got . . .

After the war I had a spell when I was obsessed with making
ice cream, as a business. It was a funny thing, a germ settled in
my mind, like a criminal who does silly things, bent things. It
was self-inflicted in a way, and it began when I was in the Home
Guard. I used to have to spend many nights on my own, at the
HQ, on the front at Porteynon. And the HQ was in an old Italian
ice cream café, and when I'd be there at night, by myself, the
idea grew on me . . . if they could do it, I'd say to myself, I'm
sure I could, this'd be easier than farming. So in 1945 I got the
tenancy of the old café from the estate, and I had a go. I went
headlong for this, and before long I had three vans selling ice
cream around the villages and the car parks in the summer. I
used to make it with fresh milk, and the people lapped it up.
They say even now they rarely find anything so good around
today. It's the fresh milk that did it, I think. It did for me in the
end, too, because I got into trouble with the police over using
fresh milk, after it had been banned for ice cream. Can you beat
that?

But there was something else working against me . . . I've
always been a religious sort of chap, and I began to resent being
such a busy-body on the Lord's Day, I never had any bells, just a
peep-peep, and the people would come running with their
dishes and their cups. But I had a dread of disturbing the service
in the church, and the peace of the Sabbath. So I gave up the ice
cream after a few years, and just in time, too, because by then
there was beginning a vicious build up of the big ice cream

makers in every village and the pre-packed stuff soon became all the rage. And now, of course, they're back to the soft stuff again. Amazing.

My father and mother both died in 1952, so I came back to the farm to help my brother. And by then I had become something of a leading spirit in music and dancing and village parties. When I was quite young I was very keen on dancing. I went to my first grand dance when I was fourteen, a big ball at Horton, one-and-six to go in. Most other dances were tanner hops. Drums and piano, honky-tonk stuff. But in this big ball I remember I met the junior teacher of the school, and I danced with her, to her great amusement. But I danced quite well for my age, and I loved it. I longed to be able to play this dance music on an accordion, but I couldn't get on with music at school. I didn't like the shape of the notes on the treble clef. I found music very tiring . . . we had a little outfit there, the boys used to squabble over playing on the drums, and there were triangles and cymbals, but it gave me no exciting interest. My poor father wanted me to have a banjo, but then he bought me a small melodion—a Getel from Hitler's Germany, 14/6. I've got it now, it's a sort of mouth organ. He could play it. I remember him rendering 'Home Sweet Home' to me in the farmyard. But what I longed for was an accordion, so my father eventually bought me one, and I had lessons from a woman in Llanmadog for four years or so. I didn't want to learn at first . . . "To hell with music", I said, "I just want to play the accordion". "Well", she said, "You'll have to learn to use your hands. Why don't you try this line here . . ." And she got me playing the first line . . . and I was astonished to find myself playing a few notes of music in the key of C, in three-four time, and doing a vamp with my left hand. I felt that was the first time I had played music. I can read it now, but I'm sorry to say I'm very slow in reading it. Very poor on sight. An easy waltz I could manage. But I picked up a lot by ear.

They needed someone like me for dances in Gower, I thought, so I got together a little outfit with piano and drums and this I ran for about ten years, till 1955. I gave that up because of late nights. One o'clock jobs, all of a run. You can't work after that sort of thing, and what with my health cracking, and trouble with the band, the bad ones beginning to drink a lot, and bad women—between outselves, I decided it wasn't a good life for me,—better for me to go steady and do village parties only. And that's what I did after that.

The village party craze began I think in Horton, in the thirties with what they called the Forum parties, for some reason, then later the Bright Hour parties, run by the chapel, once a fortnight. And that began a great period, the era of the super Village Parties, they were indescribable. Of course, in the end television came, with pictures in the home, a very exciting thing, and it killed the parties. Now it seems to me sometimes that the village hall is a dead duck, it has outlived its purpose, like the fairground. They've all had their run, and now enthusiasm isn't the same. But just after the war, the village parties reached their peak, take those in Horton and Rhossili, they were the kings, they were really great, sort of inspired, I think, by the spirit of the community. And I was proud to be part of it. I'd turn up sometimes, and they'd all seem to be keyed up, waiting for me to come and strike up a dance tune. I like to think that I gave a lot of myself to those evenings. I mustn't brag, but that's how they made me feel. They were great fun, and I used to look forward to them so much, I didn't need to note them in my diary. I used to dress up for the special parties, for the children or Christmas time, say, a cheerful sort of costume usually, a bit like a pirate, or a cossack, you know, red and green, with some silver hanging from the arms, and when I got wound up, I'd offer all I'd got. I'd play my very best, not too good perhaps, but I'd laugh, and giggle, and it would be catching, somehow.

The Gower people always used to be famous for their 'stepping' and it used to come out at times like that, some great dancing going on in the hall. They really were uplifting, those parties. People were happy, and really radiant. And I like to think that I was an inspired person, that I made them all as great as they were. Who knows? But let's be fair, a lot of it was thanks to good organisation locally. I mean, don't let's forget the refreshments. A cup of tea the like of which you could never forget, beautiful, just when you were getting dry. And marvellous sandwiches, and cakes, and trifles in a dish. I used to charge fifteen shillings for the evening, a fair little fee, mind, but don't forget, I was always stuffed with tea and good food. In the end I got sillier, and I did all the parties for nothing. In fact I used to do a few children's parties the same night, rushing from one village to another like a mad thing.

This great cycle lasted for just over ten years, then the decline set in, as I say. The spirit was lacking somehow. And all that is left of those unforgettable celebrations is the Harvest Supper. Isn't it sad? The young people, I know, have what they call Barn Dances. But those were O.K. about fifty years ago, when conditions were more primitive. It's a bit of a lark these days to open up a barn and hold a dance there. But there's nothing comfy or cosy about that, there are no toilets, no water, not very sanitary either, what with the lice and the spiders and things. Far better to dress up a bit and run a proper ball. They have a bar, of course. But that to me is the beginning of trouble. They drink till they're incapable of dancing. They smell bad, then they get cross and start their nonsense. I've had some, I know. Dreadful shame. And what do they call dancing today? God help us, I say. Just shuffling and shaking, partners getting further apart. Enjoyable in a selfish sort of way, perhaps, but I mean, real dancing is such a fantastic hobby. To do a waltz now, or a foxtrot, or a tango, or take the Lancers, God, what a dance that is, you have to have discipline. It's a controlled movement, and not just to numbers, but you move to music and to rhythm and step, and that sort of dancing you can keep up to old age—and I will do, unless I'm too tired by then to bother!

Another thing I've taken up—since the party days—is bell-ringing. Controlled movement again for you. Though there are only two bells at Porteynon Church. I've been doing it for fifteen years now, and I'm the only bell-ringer left. People in the parish tell me they always knew when I was ringing, I seem to have the knack now, though when I started I made a ridiculous mess of it. You see, with those bells, there's quite a trick to it. You have to take up the pull first, down about nine inches . . . when you start off you've got nothing, it's as if you are milking a cow, until the bell strikes the hammer. I'm Rector's Warden now, too, so I help the Rector with the church. This is good for me, because it means I hardly miss a service all the year round.

I've always had great religious feelings, you know. I am convinced that the moment I fall asleep in death, I'll be living. If you believe this, you can face death easily. And I try to be friendly with everyone, even strangers, even to love my enemies, those who disregard me. I find the spirit of Jesus very hard to resist. I've often been asked why, with my feeling for people, I'm still a bachelor. My answer to that is, "Well, you can't blame the girls, can you?" By that I meant that no girl could see enough in me to want me. I suppose that a girl acts as a mouse-trap, isn't it? And we should fall in and get caught. I did court one girl for twelve months and one for three, but nothing came of it. I see no real point in being a bachelor, mind, though it's a great life. You can come and go as you like, and you've got no one to quarrel with. I take three weeks holiday every year, and I enjoy being on my own. If you've got a wife you love, this takes up a lot of your time, doesn't it? Besides, I'm never lonely, because Jesus is always with me. I believe that sincerely. And my life is getting more and more like that every day.

PART V

The Landowners

DOROTHY ANSON (neé HELME), Hill End

My father came to Hill End in this way. He spent most of his life in the City, as director of a bank. But he was very interested in the country and he was always looking out for places to go wild-fowling, even on the Continent. Anyway he was down one day somewhere near Burry Port, excellent wild-fowling there, it seems, and looking across he could see the hills of West Gower. They told him it was even better the other side, so he went over and found they were right. So he looked around for somewhere to buy, I think he just wanted a place to go and enjoy himself, away from the family. He was from Essex, edge of Epping Forest and he had shot and fished all his life in the estuaries round there. Funny how all these places, like Gower, are very heavily preserved now, but he had acquired then a real passion for shooting. It was like this: He had an elder brother, you see, who was in the 8th Hussars and when he was in India during the Mutiny he went out one day, to shoot for the pot, but he fell into a runnah (bed of stream), and the gun went off and shot him dead. Because of that my father was not allowed to touch a gun, and his dead brother's gun was left hanging in the kitchen and no one was allowed to go near it. But one day, when he was fifteen, his father and mother were in London for the day, he took this gun down and went up into the forest to shoot a rabbit. Of course the gun was not looked after, it exploded and he lost the index finger of his right hand, his trigger finger. Still nothing deterred him from then on.

At first he came down once or twice a year—August and September he would start shooting—then in 1870 the family started coming down in April, and again in the summer until November. But my first visit must have been in August 1895. I was only a few months old and one of the first things I remember was being carried around by a donkey with panniers, I was installed on one side and there was a stone as counter-balance in the other, and a nice little awning fixed up to keep the sun off! The roads and tracks were far too rough for a perambulator, the babies were mostly carried in shawls. My nurse was a North-walian, she taught me the Lord's Prayer in Welsh and when

Bishop Owen came to Llangennith for a confirmation I had to recite it to him. I was about five then.

When we went down to Hill End there was quite a procession I remember. The butler and the footman went down first, so did my mother's maid, sometimes a nurse. And a groom brought two riding horses down, all the way from London and they were with us until we went back in November. But he always kept some cobs on the burrows nearby and we used them to get about, with me walking up all the hills! When we arrived at the station we were met by Mr Pike's landau and the carrier used to take all the luggage, which was considerable. The roads were terrible, it took about three hours to get to Hill End. The old stonemen in every village used to spend the autumn breaking stones, but as soon as we went back, the stones were put on the road, and for some years there was no roller to roll them in. I think the villagers kept their youthful looks and upright bearing because they went everywhere on foot.

Gower in those days had little contact with the outside world beyond Swansea. My mother told me that when she used to visit scattered and isolated farms, sometime in the '70s, she mentioned the Queen to one old lady, and she thought she was referring to Queen Adelaide! We had water at Hill End piped down from the hill, very, very good water it was. And lighting was candles. I remember when October came candles were lit even at breakfast time. Then came home-made electricity, about 1911. But as long as my father had his gun he was happy. Miss Talbot of Penrice gave him permission to shoot on some of the land but there was some freehold land in the villages and he used to pay the villagers for every bird he shot. Around Christmas-time he used to make up little packets of new-minted silver and present it to them. I think it was a shilling a bird. Then he used to invite all the village families who had been of service to us to a big Harvest Supper. Great fare that was. George Richards played the fiddle and later in the evening there was 'stepping'. Some of them were great steppers. I used to have to leave about eleven, and then things used to warm up and my father would tell about the pearl necklaces he'd found near the pigsties, and nonsense like that. Anyway they kept the fun up until it was time to go milking next morning.

My father really enjoyed Gower, at one time he owned all the Bay except the two glebe fields and he bought Burry Holms—he didn't want people coming "poking around", you know,—disturbing his game! But Gower is a place such that, when you get too old to walk you don't want to be there any more. And so one day he decided to leave, and he never went back—two years later he died. Gave Hill End to my brother (Colonel Helme), and the same thing happened to him. He kept on living there throughout the war and then found he couldn't get about. He was twenty-two years older than me, but now that I'm finding difficulty in getting as far as the sands myself, I quite understand their selling it off.

Of course Phil Tanner used to come down for the Harvest Supper. He really was an old scoundrel, you know. He had the evil eye, so the locals told me. He or his wife; and people were afraid of upsetting them in any way. He would always sing "The Old Grey Mare", and Mr Roberts the smith would sing his song. The same people always sang the same songs, you see.

We used to know quite a number of people. It made all the difference. Our great friends, of course, were the Bostocks of Fairyhill. Old Mrs Bostock was a sister of Mrs Matthew Arnold's. All the daughters would come and stay, too. I would get about twenty people to Hill End when I had my birthday in April. Then I used to go and have tea with certain people in the village. Parson J. D. Davies always came over to see us and we visited him regularly. I once asked him to make me a throne for my doll, I remember. He made all kinds of things with wood, you know, he had a workshop which I'd seen, so . . . anyway he said he would. Mother was very angry, "You should never ask Mr Davies to do such a thing". But he did, he built a beautiful throne with three steps up to it, an oak seat on the top, with a gold crown and a fringe round the bottom. I loved it, but it was left in Hill End with all the other things. We left some lovely Irish silver there, too. My father used to bring back a bit of silver every time he went up to London for a board meeting.

One regular visitor at that time was the weaver, Isaac Tanner.

He'd come over in August and fleeces would be put out for him
to inspect. He'd make a careful selection, including one black
one, roll them up and carry them back to his mill. Then when
we returned in April there'd be a nice roll of homespun waiting
for us. David Ace the tailor would make this up into shooting
suits for my father.

My brother used to know the villagers very well indeed. He
thought a lot of them. And there *was* something different about
these people. They had the most exquisite manners, natural
good manners. I remember him saying: "They treat you exactly
as if you were royalty". Why, I don't know. Something in the
stock, I believe. One odd custom that was kept up was that
when they died, those who were freeholders were always
carried over their portion of freehold property on the way to the
church. Of course no one was taken except by bearers, the
whole way, maybe miles and miles, with relief sets of bearers,
because the roads were too bad for a wheeled vehicle of any sort.
And in my time there was another thing the farmers did: all the
cows were dried off in the autumn so there was no fresh milk all
the winter. We lived on that Nestlé's stuff in tins. Until the
cows calved next spring. I believe that's why many had such
bad teeth. I know all the girls who worked for us had to have a
new set of teeth by the time they were seventeen. On the
whole, farming was very poor. Mangels, good size, was about
all that did well in those days.

The practical intelligence of Rhossili people always amazed
my father, sea-faring types a lot of them. But I remember him
saying how remarkable they were at lifting weights, for
instance, with boats and things, he had never seen it done
anywhere else. And with machinery they are very ingenious I
believe. You know, keeping an ancient tractor going for long
after someone else would have scrapped it. They have a feeling
for things when they're not going right. I hope that doesn't die
out. I don't think it will.

My brother used to do a lot of singing in the villages. He used
to sing in the choir at Winchester when he had a very good
soprano voice. But it was forced for too long, and it never
reformed—so he started whistling his songs. He had a very keen

ear, you see. All those soprano songs with a lot of coloraturo in them, he whistled them all, very, very good he was. Until the War, that is, then he got a piece of shrapnel in his lungs, so that he couldn't take a deep breath, and he gradually had to give up the whistling. Such a pity. To hear him whistle 'Bohème' or 'Lo Hear the Gentle Lark' was really something. Everywhere he went he kept people going as far as music was concerned. And in 1924 he put together a 'Gower Pageant' in Penrice Park that was a really memorable event in the lives of the people, and it's been talked about ever since.

CHRISTOPHER METHUEN-CAMPBELL

Landed gentleman-farmer

The story of how I came into the Penrice Estate is rather a sad one, really. My grandmother, Lady Blytheswood, had given over the estate to my mother, in order to avoid death duties and to make sure of continuity. But my mother died before her, in 1948. So the whole object was defeated and eventually double death duties had to be paid. At one time we thought Penrice would have to be sold: my father didn't like South Wales very much and other death duties in Scotland had to be paid. So almost all the Gower farms were sold to the existing tenants. I think they made a frightful mistake in selling so many of them. Because when the estate came to me I only seemed to have the worthless bits, it was a completely uneconomic proposition. I was under age, anyway, and didn't have any sense at all. Now, of course, the worthless bits have turned out to be profitable, like car parks and beaches, and I have bought some land back, which gives me about 1200 acres of farm land.

Being Lord of the Manor doesn't mean a lot since Courts Leet finished, but it gives us some very unusual rights: for one thing we are the actual owners of the foreshore. In most places this is vested in the Crown, but in a few spots—St Michael's Mount is another example—the Lord of the Manor has flotsam and jet-

sam and wrecking rights. But although I'm lord of fourteen
manors in Gower, this hasn't been a lot of use to me! There are,
of course, rights over manorial wastes and the commons and
rights of grazing, and turbary (cutting of turf), these could be
relevant today to some degree. And I get a small income for
telegraph and electricity poles and telephone kiosks. Big stuff!
And I can even charge someone to take a boat onto a beach. This
is a good thing in a way, because it gives me a lot of control over,
say, anyone making a nuisance on the sands. And it's a godsend
from the conservation point of view, especially at Oxwich.

When my grandmother inherited it from Miss Talbot in
1920, it was an estate of 30,000 acres, but all she wanted to do
was keep everything as it was. It was because of this policy of
stagnation that so much of Gower remained unspoiled, rather
than through any positive intention to conserve it. I suppose
really that until the Second World War it was all run more or
less as it had been since the 18th century. When it was left to
me there were still forty or fifty employees, even a clerk of
works, and an agent, Pritchard, who was God Almighty on a
white horse. For a long time it had suffered from having two
women at the head, one after the other, with no business sense
at all. They didn't put up the rents, they didn't do the repairs
they should have, a lot of the property was in a very bad state,
there was no modern approach at all. But there was one very
real, rather extraordinary thing which still persisted,
something that always used to be part of the countryside,—
and that was a pride in the land, in the people, and in the estate,
the sort of cohesion that grew up between landlord and tenant,
and an easiness of approach from both sides. It was a sort of
partnership, that has now completely vanished. Gower was
unique in some ways, since it was a unit with a tradition, even a
language, all its own.

One hears awful stories about the rest of Glamorgan, with
often English landlords and Welsh-speaking tenants, but I'm
sure that Penrice over the years has not been so anglicised as it
could have become. All my predecessors loved Gower—you
can see that from the family letters over the centuries—and the
tenants, naturally, always had their full support. If they were

Penrice Castle, 1915.

good tenants, of course. One did look down to some extent on the outsider. The agent, Pritchard, obviously didn't share this philosophy, and from what I hear he was the worst agent any landlord could have had in Wales. He wasn't very efficient, far too old-fashioned, but he did keep things together in some sort of cohesion, I suppose.

It would have been a very interesting exercise to have handled the big estate, which was losing about £15,000 a year when my mother died. This was paid for by our estate in Scotland. Anyway, now it makes a bit of money for me, and enables me to repair this place and the farm buildings. For fifteen years I was farming in Shropshire. I did a degree in Agriculture, and one of the reasons I came down here was that I couldn't bear to think of the house being sold up, it was a most wonderful place to carry on my main interests, which were gardening and farming and natural history and I thought I could do some useful work in conservation. I found the attitude of the local farmers very encouraging. I probably got on better with them as the ex-landlord than I would have as their landlord. I must say I found very little resentment towards the old régime, though of course they had had little to complain about, their rate of rent had been very gentle. It is interesting that the situation had been more or less static for six or seven hundred years, and that it could have survived so long. No, I think *I* was more critical of the old estate than the tenants had been. I was very harsh at times, believe me.

As a child I had learned to love the place and respect the past too much to want to break completely with it, so if the whole estate had come to me I'd have simply tried to be more business-like and more objective in the running of it, a lot harder, or at least firmer, at the outset anyway. Obviously there was some measure of resentment against Penrice, but if a landlord plays his part efficiently, he will stand more chance of being a respected partner. There is a lot to be said for a tenancy, as long as they and you speak the same language and you don't get bogged down in the last century.

In my present position I do feel I am free to follow my own interests. I'm not the squire, I'm known now throughout

Gower by my Christian name. I can talk to anybody and they can talk to me, which is not always easy in England. One can be oneself, and one must be. Sometimes I think that Penrice has been a millstone round my neck. I am aware that I am leading a completely archaic existence. But at least I can carry on being a farmer. I have a market garden here, and I breed cows. I've got to earn some money anyway. I don't believe I benefit from any aura or glamour of Penrice, not any more, they know me too well. With newcomers, yes, you can feel they have a certain awe in meeting me, but it's not me, it's the house. I have become very interested in anything that goes on in the villages, in the people, too. The level of intelligence is far higher than that of the country people in the parts of England I know. They have a lot of pride, and self-possession, they're independent, with a lot of talent, and a sense of humour. They had security, of course, under the old estate, and that may have helped them to blossom a little, who knows?

I have become deeply concerned about the countryside as a whole, and its conservation as a working entity, for future generations to enjoy something of what I enjoy and what my ancestors once enjoyed. As a leisure area Gower is being subjected to pressures from all sides, and one recent development worries me a lot, because it is so well-intentioned. The increase in educational visits, I mean. We have Field Study Centres, Adventure Schools, quite a few school hostels, and unless their activities can be co-ordinated, a lot of damage can be done. In some cases parties change every week, they come from far and near, and some have shown themselves to be not a little inconsiderate. One group for example started clearing a wide footpath through a woodland without realising that it was a Nature Reserve. Sensitive areas must be protected. Like Oxwich. I have suggested that universities could adopt Oxwich as an outdoor laboratory. Then there would be strict control by specialists. There are there, for example, fourteen different habitats which a student can study. All this is precious. The heronry in Penrice Park for example, which is part of the Nature Reserve, is over 150 years old. I think the would-be experts are more dangerous than the casual holiday-makers. In the sand dune areas, erosion is a great problem and I'd like to do something about that. I'd also like to get the Department of the Environment to look after the old castle in the park. And I'd like to do some re-building of Oxwich Castle. The park itself of course is man-made, artificial,—it is marvellous, too, but it is less vulnerable. I've always tried to get the park used for Gower activities. The Gower Show started here about 1910, and that was the right idea. More recently I've let it be used for horse-jumping events, and I've even brought in motor-racing, but that didn't work terribly well, they left a lot of mess. I find it fun to see a lot of people enjoying themselves here. The house itself has in a way always been available to the public, though we don't advertise this. It is too small to cope with crowds, but if anyone wants to come and see the Castle, they can always make an appointment. In this way we only get the people who are really interested, rather than the gawpers. Same thing goes for the Nature Reserve and the heronry.

When I want to be left alone, which is often, I am to be found in the garden. I really love it there, this part of the world is a marvellous spot to garden in, you really have got an extraordinary climate for it. Eucalyptus has no difficulty in flourishing here, and I've got a whole forest of mimosa.

I often think of how things were when I was a boy staying here. So typical of Penrice in those days. There were five men working in the gardens, and we were not allowed to touch a thing. My grandmother wouldn't allow anything to be cut; so gradually the gardens encroached on the house and no one could walk down the paths! Not a branch was allowed to come away. Typical of the life-style followed at Penrice, dominated by two women . . .

Same with the house itself. When Miss Talbot died in 1918 she left my grandmother three and a half thousand to spend on the house. But my grandmother, being my grandmother, couldn't bring herself to spend a penny of it. So when she died, we had to pay death duties on the three and a half thousand as well. And this left the house in such a state that the architect I consulted said that given ten more years the place would have fallen down on its own. So you can imagine . . . we had to take the roof off, at one time you could see the sky from the ground floor here. Most of the rooms had not been decorated since the 1880s and were crumbling to bits. Dry rot everywhere. All the carpets except one had to be destroyed. The interesting thing was that the nineteenth century hadn't touched it at all, it had missed the Georgian period altogether! We found a lot of the old furniture in a stable, all in pieces. We were lucky enough to get a lot of that repaired, in the 60s. Anyway, I think we've saved the house for another hundred years, if we're lucky.

When I was a child the house seemed full of servants, although everything was very shabby and tatty. There were, in fact, twenty then on the indoor and outdoor staff. I remember a very grand housekeeper called Mrs Sweft, she had four house-maids under her. And a nice cook, Mrs Slaughter, with three kitchen maids. There was a chauffeur, and an under-chauffeur. He was a Mr Gibbs, a wonderful chap, he'd been trained by Rolls-Royce before World War One. There was a butler, with two footmen and a boot-boy. And I'll never forget old Arthur (Jenkins). He looked after the oil-lamps. It was the middle of the last war before electricity came as far as this. And because Arthur was a teetotaller he used to look after the beer—there were always two or three barrels of beer kept outside the back door. There were about eighteen people working inside the house in those days, including a house carpenter. Heaven knows what he did. Though there was a lot of furniture to look after, and it used to be polished beautifully. When I was a child in the nursery here a little girl used to come at half past six in the morning to clear the grate, polish it, lay a fire and light it. We always had a fire in every single fireplace in the house, even the hall. Very nice and cosy, if you happened to be near one. Heating the place is no problem nowadays. We just haven't got any heating, apart from the odd strategically placed fire.

The kitchen was huge and Victorian, and it was in the servants quarters. The butler would carve the joint there, and they had four large tables to set out the food. This would be brought to the living room, about two hundred yards away, in a big hay box by the footman and put into a hot cupboard. In the living room stood Mr Brown the butler, and he would serve it out. It was always stone cold. But they didn't seem to eat a lot, my grandmother rarely ate at all. Neither did they drink very much. Though there is a fine cellar here, but it's a long time since it had any wine in it!

While we were re-doing the house we had to deal with an odd situation in the rooms under the roof. We had noticed that the attic ceilings were all apt to drip with something like honey. We found it *was* honey, and when we stripped the ceilings we had the delightful task of taking away ten tons of it. But it was no good at all, it was all black and rotten, had been there for ages. Wild Welsh bees had settled there and had been coming back and fore ever since the house was built, I should think. We've still got bees in the roof here, they come in through one chimney, and it's an awful job when we have to clean the chimneys.

We have a pretty archaic method of doing this, too, cleaning the chimneys. We take a big round lead ball, like a cannon ball, and this is lowered down from the highest point, taking with it a holly bush tied behind. Honestly. It's by far the best way. It ends up in the grate in the room, and the holly bush is then pulled down the chimney. An ideal thing, a holly bush, nice and stiff and takes all the soot with it. I understand it was a well-known method of chimney sweeps in the old days.

Anyway, the days of a houseful of servants are no more, thank Heaven. We now have two dailies to see to everything. They come in for a couple of hours in the mornings, they know the house well, and they keep it very nicely. What happens when they go, God only knows! Apart from that, we look after ourselves.

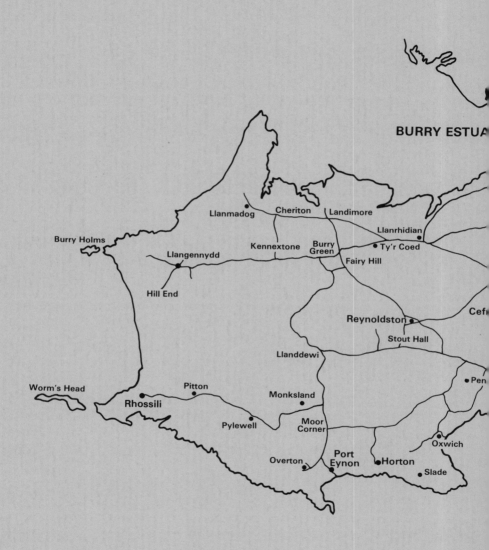

BURRY ESTUA

Burry Holms

Llanmadog

Cheriton

Landimore

Llanrhidian

Kennextone

Burry
Green

Ty'r Coed

Llangennydd

Fairy Hill

Hill End

Reynoldston

Cefn

Stout Hall

Llanddewi

Worm's Head

Pitton

Monksland

Pen

Rhossili

Pylewell

Moor
Corner

Oxwich

Overton

Port
Eynon

Horton

Slade

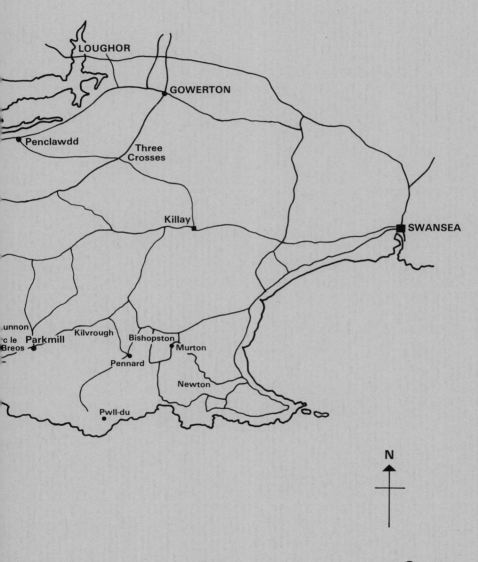

LOUGHOR

GOWERTON

Penclawdd

Three
Crosses

Killay

SWANSEA

unnon
c le
Breos

Parkmill

Kilvrough

Bishopston

Murton

Pennard

Newton

Pwll-du

N

G 81